An Introduction

A quarter of a century may have passed since the sun finally set on the British Phantom force, but the type retains its iconic reputation with those who flew it, worked on it or simply admired it from afar. *KEY - Duncan Cubitt*

British Phantoms (1967 to 1992)

Welcome to our tribute to one of the most loved fighter aircraft ever to serve with the British military. Featuring many unseen photographs and first-hand accounts the following pages trace the history of the McDonnell Douglas F-4 Phantom II in British service.

It is hard to believe that 25 years have passed since the RAF retired its 'Phinal Phantom' in October 1992.

The British version of the Phantom was an aircraft designed essentially to a Royal Navy specification. It also had extra 'tweaks' made to it in an attempt both win political favour and enable it to be produced in Britain so as to keep the unions happy.

The result was an aeroplane that was vastly more expensive than an 'off the shelf' Phantom with inferior performance in many aspects. Nevertheless, the first examples were delivered to the Navy's Fleet Air Arm in 1967 and the RAF accepted its production airframes the following year.

In a twist of fate the Royal Navy was eventually to find itself bereft of an aircraft carrier capable of operating the big supersonic fleet defence fighter and in 1978 the final Fleet Air Arm Phantoms were handed over to the RAF.

Considering it was an aircraft the RAF never really wanted the Phantom went on to have a distinguished air force career. It was flown operationally in RAF Germany during the Cold War, flew in defence of Cyprus during the Gulf War and provided essential fast jet cover for the Falkland Islands from the mid 1980s.

But all things come to an end, and in 1992 the last examples were flown into retirement, with the majority of them succumbing to the scrapper's axe in order to meet the demands of post Glasnost arms treaties.

Today, the handful of surviving Phantoms remember the important role this big fighter had in the defence of Britain and its overseas territories.

I hope you enjoy the articles in this eulogy to the British Phantom, many of which include input from former aircrew and ground crew.

Stephen Bridgewater
Stamford, October 2017

Front cover artwork courtesy of Antonis Karidis

Phantom © Key Publishing 2017

Editor: Stephen Bridgewater **Sub Editor:** Rebecca Gibbs **Proof Reading:** Jamie Ewan **Design and Layout** Paul Silk. **Group Editor:** Nigel Price
Publisher and Managing Director Adrian Cox. **Executive Chairman** Richard Cox. **Commercial Director** Ann Saundry.
Distribution Seymour Distribution Ltd +44 (0)20 7429 4000. **Printing** Warners (Midlands) PLC, The Maltings, Manor Lane, Bourne, Lincs PE10 9PH.
ISBN 978 1 912205 06 6   *All images via the Key Publishing Archive unless stated*

All rights reserved. Reproduction in whole or in part and in any form whatsoever is strictly prohibited without the prior permission of the Publisher. Whilst every care is taken with submissions, the Publisher cannot be held responsible for any loss or damage incurred. All items submitted for publication are subject to our terms and conditions which are regularly updated without prior notice and downloadable from www.keypublishing.com. We are unable to guarantee the *bona fides* of any of our advertisers. Readers are strongly recommended to take their own precautions before parting with any information or item of value, including, but not limited to, money, manuscripts, photographs or personal information in response to any advertisements within this publication.

Published by Key Publishing Ltd, PO Box 100, Stamford, Lincs PE19 1XQ.
Tel: +44 (0) 1780 755131. Fax: +44 (0) 1780 757261. Website: www.keypublishing.com

CONTENTS British Phantoms

Crown Copyright

3 Introduction

6 The Flying Anvil - Sixty Phabulous Years
In May 2018 it will be 60 years since the McDonnell Douglas F-4 Phantom first took to the air. The aircraft has enjoyed a remarkable career and it remains in service with the several air arms around the globe. We look back at 60 Phabulous Years.

12 British Phantoms - On Her Majesty's Service
The Phantom would go on to be one of Britain's most capable strike, attack and air defence aircraft – but in the early days it is was an aeroplane that the British forces really didn't want.

22 Flying the Phantom
Air Commodore Rick Peacock-Edwards CBE AFC FRAeS FCIM flew the English Electric Lightning, McDonnell Douglas F-4 Phantom and Panavia Tornado F.2/F.3 during a stellar RAF career. He explains to Steve Bridgewater why the Phantom was a real war machine.

30 The Admiralty's Phantoms
From the outset the British Phantoms were designed to meet a mostly naval orientated specification. The Fleet Air Arm operated the type for just over ten years, during which time they frequently deployed aboard HMS *Ark Royal*.

38 Fighting the Phantom
Former Phantom navigator Ian Black recalls his detachments to the ACMI ranges at Decimomannu, where he got the opportunity to dogfight the aircraft against opponents as diverse as the F-104 Starfighter and the F-15 Eagle.

46 The Silent Battle
Former RAF Phantom navigator Dave Gledhill reveals the type's now declassified Electronic Warfare capabilities.

54 "You Fight Like You Train"
The old adage 'You fight like you train' has never been truer than in RAF Germany. Exercises at all levels allowed crews to hone their skills to be ready to respond to any contingency. Dave Gledhill reveals what life was like while operating the iconic jet during a Cold War air defence exercise.

Airspace Images

60 Black Mike
Phantom XV582 was the first of the British Phantoms to exceed 5,000 flying hours but it also set a world speed record and is famed for wearing one of the most dramatic special schemes to ever adorn a Phantom. Today, 'Black Mike' is a rare survivor with an exciting future.

64 Big Cat Hunting
The RAF Phantom fleet only scored one air-to-air victory – but it was not a celebrated event, as Ian Black reveals.

70 Flying Colours
Throughout their career RAF Phantoms have been adorned with some spectacular colour schemes. Here is just a small selection of the some of the most decorative.

72 Phantom Losses
We provide an overview of the most notable losses and incidents incurred by Fleet Air Arm and Royal Air Force Phantom squadrons.

76 Falklands Phantoms
The Argentine invasion of the Falkland Islands in 1982 revealed a weakness in British air defences. Soon after the conflict RAF Phantoms found a new home at a small South Atlantic airfield and 1435 Flight was reborn.

82 Phantom vs Tornado
The RAF Phantom fleet was ultimately replaced by the Panavia Tornado F.3 in the early 1990s. Not only was Ian Black privileged to fly both types – he's one of the few people to have flown against an RAF Phantom in an RAF Tornado. He explains how he fared.

88 Phantom Phase Out
By the beginning of the 1990s the RAF Phantom fleet was nearing the end of its life. Twenty-five years on from the type's retirement we look at those final days and the last salute.

96 The Survivors
Of the 170 Phantoms flown by the UK military just a handful remain into the 21st century. Here we present a breakdown of the lucky few survivors.

The Flying Anvil
Sixty Phabulous Years

The second prototype YF4H-1 (BuNo 142260) carrying high visibility markings during the test flying campaign in March 1959. *US Navy* **Inset above:** The Phantom's emblem is a whimsical cartoon ghost called 'The Spook', which was created by McDonnell Douglas technical artist Tony Wong for use on squadron patches.

In May 2018 it will be 60 years since the McDonnell Douglas F-4 Phantom first took to the air. The aircraft has enjoyed a remarkable career and it remains in service with the several air arms around the globe. We look back at 60 'Phabulous' Years.

'Snoopy', 'Spooky', 'Double Ugly', the 'Flying Brick', the 'Rhino', the 'St Louis Slugger', the 'Iron Pig' or the 'Flying Anvil' – no matter what unflattering nicknames the McDonnell Douglas F-4 Phantom II has been given during six decades of operation, it can justifiably lay claim to being an aviation legend.

The aircraft's history dates back to 1952 when Dave Lewis was appointed as McDonnell Douglas (MDD) Chief of Aerodynamics and Preliminary Design Manager. Lewis found himself at the helm of a department that had no aircraft design, so he launched an internal study which concluded that the US Navy had the greatest need for a new aircraft type; specifically a supersonic attack fighter.

Lewis' team initially began by revising MDD's existing F3H Demon to give it better performance. The resultant 'Super Demon' had a projected top speed of Mach 1.97 and was pitched to the US Navy in September 1953. However, although the Navy liked the concept it felt the upcoming Grumman XF9F-9 and Vought XF8U-1 Crusader already satisfied the need for a supersonic fighter.

The MDD design was therefore reworked into a single-seat all-weather fighter-bomber with eleven external weapons hardpoints and on October 18, 1954 a 'letter of intent' was placed for two prototypes under the YAH-1 designation.

Work began in earnest and mock-ups were constructed but everything changed on May 29 the following year when a small contingent of government officials arrived at the MDD offices and, within an hour, presented the company with an entirely new set of highly detailed requirements.

It was felt that the new Douglas A-4 Skyhawk fulfilled the Navy's single-seat fighter bomber role and the current need was for a two-seat fleet defence fighter capable of a hitherto unheard of mission: a 300-mile (464km) radius of action combined with two hours Combat Air Patrol (CAP) on station, during which the jet would need to detect, engage and destroy enemy aircraft.

XF4H-1 Prototype

The YAH-1 design was therefore refined to accommodate the second crewmember. It also lost the internal guns, which were replaced by four semi-recessed AAM-N-6a Sparrow III radar-guided missiles under the fuselage.

As in the company's earlier McDonnell F-101 Voodoo, the two General Electric J79-GE-8 engines sat low in the fuselage to maximise internal fuel capacity and ingested air through fixed geometry intakes. In addition, air intakes were equipped with variable geometry ramps to regulate airflow to the engines at supersonic speeds.

The thin-section wing had a leading edge sweep of 45° and was equipped with blown flaps for better low-speed handling. Wind tunnel testing revealed lateral instability issues that required the addition of 5° dihedral to the wings – but this would have meant redesigning the entire titanium central section of the aircraft so engineers compromised and angled up only the outer portions of the wings by 12° (which averaged out to the required 5° over the entire wingspan).

The all-moving tailplane was also given 23° of anhedral to improve control at high angles of attack while still keeping the tailplane clear of the engine exhaust. To accommodate carrier operations a sturdy undercarriage was also fitted,

The first XF4H-1 test aircraft (BuNo 142259) on its maiden flight on May 27, 1958. A hydraulic problem prevented the landing gear from retracting on that sortie. *US Navy*

complete with a twin-wheeled nose leg that could extend by 20in (51cm) to increase angle of attack during deck take-offs.

The US Navy ordered two XF4H-1 test aircraft and five YF4H-1 pre-production examples on July 25, 1955 and the first example (BuNo 142259) took to the skies on May 27, 1958 with Robert C Little at the controls. A hydraulic problem prevented the landing gear from retracting but the problem was soon rectified and flight-testing progressed quickly.

Trials resulted in major modifications being made to the air intakes, including the addition of 12,500 holes to 'bleed' the slow-moving boundary layer air from the surface of each intake ramp. Subsequent aircraft also featured splitter plates to divert the boundary layer away from the engine intakes.

In September 1958 the YF4H-1 moved to Edwards AFB, California for service trials and the following month it was joined by a second example, BuNo 142260, for a 'fly-off' competition against the XF8U-3 Crusader III. The Navy specifically wanted a second crew member to reduce workload so the single-seat Crusader lost out to the MDD aircraft and in December an order for 23 development aircraft was placed.

'Second' Phantom

MDD had traditionally named its jet aircraft after ghosts, spirits and 'dark happenings' (Voodoo, Demon, Goblin, Banshee etc) and some thought was initially given to calling the production version of the YF4H-1 the 'Satan.' Conversely, company founder Jim McDonnell proposed the name 'Mithras' – relating to the Persian god of light.

In the end, a less controversial title was chosen and the new aircraft was named after MDD's (and the US Navy's) first-ever jet aircraft – the revolutionary FH-1 Phantom.

The new aircraft was therefore officially named the Phantom II as part of the manufacturer's 20th anniversary celebrations at St Louis, Missouri on July 3, 1959.

The US Navy initially operated the Phantom as the F4H-1 and received 45 of these J79-GE-2-powered machines. On December 30, 1960, the VF-121 *Pacemakers* at NAS Miramar became the first Phantom unit although none of its F4H-1Fs saw combat and most ended up as test or training aircraft.

In a major boost to MDD's order book it was decided that the USAF would also operate the Phantom in large numbers. This was as a result of Defense Secretary Robert McNamara's push to create a unified fighter for all branches of the military. Unlike the navy's focus

" Some thought was given to calling the production version the 'Satan' "

on interception, the USAF wanted a fighter-bomber but the Phantom still won the Operation *Highspeed* fly-off against the Convair F-106 Delta Dart in January 1962.

As part of McNamara's 1962 unification of designations the F4H Phantom became the universally known as the F-4 – with the naval version designated F-4A (later F-4B) and the USAF machines being F-4Cs. The first USAF Phantom flew on May 27, 1963 and exceeded Mach 2 on its maiden flight.

Navy Phantom

The first 'definitive' Navy Phantom was the F-4B variant, which was delivered to the US Navy and US Marine Corps from 1961. Power came from the uprated J79-GE-8, -8A and -8B engines producing of 10,900lb/thrust (16,950lb/thrust in reheat) and the aircraft also benefited from improved Westinghouse APQ-72 radar, a Texas Instruments AAA-4 Infra-red search and track pod and an AN/AJB-3 bombing system. The first F-4B flew on March 25, 1961 and 649 were delivered; the first being received by VF-121 *Pacemakers* at NAS Miramar.

The VF-74 *Be-Devilers* at NAS Oceana became the first deployable Phantom squadron when it received its F4H-1s (F-4Bs) on July 8, 1961 and the unit had completed carrier qualifications by October 1961. The type's first full carrier deployment took place aboard the USS *Forrestal* between August 1962 and March 1963.

McDonnell's mock up of the proposed F3H Super Demon, seen at St Louis in 1954. *US Navy*

THE FLYING ANVIL

Operation *LANA*: To celebrate the 50th anniversary of Naval Aviation F4H-1F Phantoms flew across the continental USA on May 24, 1961 as part of Operation *LANA* (L is the Roman numeral for 50 and ANA stood for Anniversary of Naval Aviation). The fastest aircraft completed the trip in 2 hours and 47 minutes averaging 869.74mph – including several aerial refuellings. *US Navy*

The F-4B was ultimately replaced in US Navy service by the F-4J variant, which had both improved air-to-air and ground attack capability as well as uprated powerplants. A total of 522 were delivered between 1966 and 1972 and thanks to its Westinghouse AN/AWG-10 Fire Control System the F-4J was the first fighter in the world with operational look-down/shoot-down capability.

The Phantom's real weakness in combat was the tell-tale smoke from its J79 engines so 288 F-4Bs were later upgraded to F-4N standard as part of Project *Bee Line*. These used J79-GE-17 variants of the engine featuring smokeless combustors.

The 265 F-4Js that were similarly modified became F-4S variants. These also had an AWG-10B radar with digitised circuitry for improved reliability, a Honeywell AN/AVG-8 Visual Target Acquisition Set (the world's first operational Helmet Sighting System) as well as airframe reinforcement and leading edge slats for enhanced manoeuvring.

It was F-4Bs from the USS *Constellation* that made the first Phantom combat sortie of the Vietnam War. This took place on August 5, 1964 as part of a bomber escort missions during Operation *Pierce Arrow* and the type would have to wait until April 9, 1965 before it gained its first air-to-air victory. Lt Terence M Murphy and Ensign Ronald Fegan were flying an F-4B from VF-96 Fighting Falcons that day when they shot down a Chinese Mikoyan Gurevich MiG-17 *Fresco*. The Phantom was then shot down, possibly by a MiG's guns or by an AIM-7 Sparrow missile fired by one of its wingmen.

During the war, US Navy Phantom squadrons participated in 84 combat tours with F-4Bs, F-4Js, and F-4Ns. Navy crews claimed 40 air-to-air victories at a cost of 73 Phantoms lost in combat (seven to enemy aircraft, 13 to SAMs, and 53 to AAA). An additional 54 were lost in accidents during the conflict.

The first Phantoms to enter service with the US Navy were F-4B variants. This VF-111 aircraft is dropping a stick of bombs during a mission over Vietnam. *US Navy*

The Phantom remained in US Navy service for many years and it was not until March 1986 than an F-4S belonging to the VF-151 *Vigilantes*, became the last active duty Navy Phantom to launch from an aircraft carrier. A year later the last of the Naval Reserve-operated F-4S aircraft were replaced by F-14A Tomcat but the Navy's QF-4 target drones operated by the Naval Air Warfare Center at NAS Point Mugu, California soldiered on as late as 2004.

The US Marine Corps (USMC) received its first Phantoms in June 1962 when F-4Bs joined the VMFA-314 *Black Knights* MCAS El Toro, California. The first USMC Phantoms to see service in Vietnam were from VMFA-531 *Gray Ghosts,* which were assigned to Da Nang airbase from May 1965, initially to provide air defence. However, they soon began close air support missions (CAS) and USMC F-4 pilots claimed three enemy MiGs (two while on exchange duty with the USAF) at the cost of 75 aircraft lost in combat, mostly to ground fire.

The F-4 continued to equip USMC fighter-attack squadrons throughout the 1960s, 70s and 80s and into the early 1990s until they were replaced by the F/A-18 Hornet.

Air Force Phantoms

For its initial USAF trials the F-4 had been designated the F-110 Spectre but when the service adopted the type it reverted to the standard F-4 Phantom name.

Although the F-4 had been designed for the US Navy it was the USAF that became the largest Phantom user and the

A VF-74 F-4B takes off in 1961. *US Navy*

USAF F-4B Phantoms return from a mission over South East Asia during the Vietnam War. *USAF Museum*

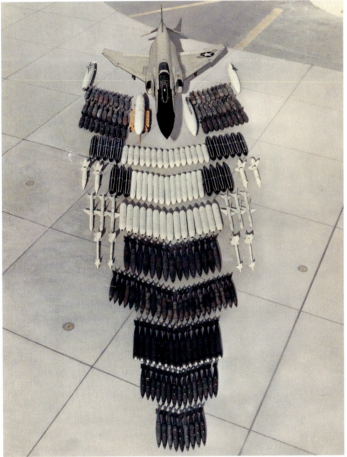

The Phantom could carry a greater bomb load than the heavy four-engined World War Two bombers such as the Avro Lancaster. *KEY Collection*

The first squadron of F-4 Wild Weasel aircraft deployed to Vietnam in October 1972 to help jam enemy radars. USAF Phantoms remained in service long enough to see further combat during Operation *Desert Storm* in 1991 and the F-4G was the only aircraft in the USAF inventory equipped for the Suppression of Enemy Air Defenses role. *KEY Collection*

The West German Luftwaffe operated a significant fleet of F-4F Phantoms in Europe and F-4Es in the USA; the latter involved in crew training. *KEY – Steve Fletcher*

first examples to arrive in Vietnam were F-4Cs from the 555th Tactical Fighter Squadron *Triple Nickel*, which arrived in December 1964.

The first USAF Phantom air-to-air victory of the war came on July 10, 1965 when F-4Cs of the 45th TFS, 15th TFW shot down North Vietnamese MiG-17s using AIM-9 Sidewinder missiles. The following April, an F-4C from the 480th TFS scored the first US aerial victory over a North Vietnamese MiG-21 *Fishbed*.

USAF Reconnaissance RF-4Cs made their debut in Vietnam on October 30, 1965, flying hazardous post-strike reconnaissance missions.

Two years later, in June 1967, the USAF's dedicated F-4D variant started arriving in theatre. Whereas the F-4C was essentially identical to the Navy's F-4B, the 'D' version was tailored specifically for the air force. The new jet carried AIM-4 Falcon missiles (in place of the AIM-9 Sidewinder), which were designed to shoot down heavy bombers. However, in reality they proved to be both unreliable and unsuitable for the job in Vietnam so by 1968 the F-4D had reverted to Sidewinders. By 1972 the aircraft had been modified to accept the new AIM-7E-2 'Dogfight Sparrow'. In October 1972 the first squadron of F-4C Wild Weasel aircraft deployed to the theatre to help jam enemy radars.

The USAF Phantoms performed both air superiority and ground attack roles in Vietnam but when the Republic F-105 Thunderchief fleet suffered severe attrition, the F-4's bombing role increased dramatically.

During the war in Vietnam some 445 USAF Phantom fighter-bombers were lost with 370 of those in combat and 193 of those over North Vietnam itself. A further 83 RF-4Cs were lost (72 in combat) taking the total USAF Phantom losses to 528. Combined with US Navy and USMC attrition a total of 761 Phantoms were lost in the Vietnam War.

USAF Phantoms remained in service long enough to see further combat during

THE FLYING ANVIL

A formation of US Navy Phantoms from Air Test and Evaluation Squadron VX-4 and the Naval Missile Center at China Lake, California in flight. Of these, aircraft QF-4B BuNo 148365 was written off at China Lake on January 31, 1974; F-4B BuNo 150435 was eventually scrapped and the two F-4Js (BuNo 153783 BuNo 153795) were both sold to the RAF in 1984 becoming ZE351 and ZE354 respectively. *US Navy*

Operation *Desert Storm* in 1991. A total of 24 F-4G Wild Weasel Vs and six RF-4Cs were deployed to the region and the F-4G was the only aircraft in the USAF inventory equipped for the Suppression of Enemy Air Defenses (SEAD) role.

In spite of flying almost daily missions, only one RF-4C and one F-4G were lost during the conflict – and only two members of crew lost their lives.

The F-4G was to be the final version of the Phantom to be operated by the USAF and the last examples were retired by the 561st Fighter Squadron in March 1996.

Like the Navy, the USAF also operated QF-4 target drones and these flew on until December 2016 – officially bringing to a close more than 55 years of US Phantom flying.

Export Operators

It was obvious to MDD from the outset that the Phantom had great export potential and the type would ultimately go on to serve with the air arms of eleven other nations around the world.

The first country to order the type was Great Britain [Ed: see page 12], which received 50 F-4K variants, 116 F-4Ms and a further 15 F-4J(UK) examples as a later 'add-on' order.

Other operators included Australia – which operated 24 as a stop-gap aircraft on loan in 1971–72 pending the arrival of General Dynamics F-111s – as well as Egypt, Germany, Greece, Iran, Israel, Japan, South Korea, Spain and Turkey.

The West German Luftwaffe operated a total of 175 F-4Fs, ten F-4Es and 88 RF-4Es from 1971. Germany was one of the most prolific Phantom customers and operated the type beyond unification until 2013.

The first Phantoms, 56 F-4s and six RF-4Es arrived for the Hellenic Air Force in 1971 and a small number of the former still serve in Greece with the 117th Combat Wing (the final RF-4s were retired in May 2017).

Spain acquired its Phantoms via the US Mutual Defense Aid Program and between 1971–72 a total of 36 ex-USAF F-4Cs were delivered – these being the only C models ever exported. Further examples followed and the Spanish Air Force would ultimately operate 58 F-4C and RF-4Cs, finally retiring the type in 2002.

The Turkish Air Force operated the F-4E and RF-4E variant and more than 230 examples were ultimately delivered – many of them ex-USAF airframes, provided in the early 1990s as a 'thank you' for use the use of Turkish bases during Operation *Desert Storm*. The type remains in extensive use within Turkey.

Israel received its first F-4E Phantoms in September 1969 and the type saw almost immediate combat with an Egyptian MiG-21 downed on November 11. During the Arab–Israeli

A Turkish Air Force F4E Phantom II takes off from Third Air Force Base Konya, Turkey, during Exercise *Anatolian Eagle* in 2014. *Crown Copyright – SAC Helen Farrer MoD*

The Hellenic Air Force and Turkish Air Force are now the only Phantom operators in Europe. *KEY Collection*

The USA provided 35 ex-USAF F-4Es to Egypt under the 1977 Peace Pharaoh agreement. *USAF Museum*

wars, Israeli F-4Es scored several aerial victories against Arab aircraft and the type had further successes during the later Yom Kippur War. Over the decade Israeli Phantoms suffered at least 55 combat losses but accounted for 116.5 claimed air victories.

The Egyptian Air Force's first encounter with the Phantom was when it was on the receiving end of the attention from Israeli examples during the War of Attrition and the 1973 Yom Kippur War. Later, the USA provided 35 ex-USAF F-4Es to Egypt under the 1977 Peace Pharaoh agreement and the air arm used them with significant success.

The Shah of Iran ordered Phantoms in the 1960s and 225 F-4Ds, F-4Es and RF-4Es were ultimately delivered to the nation and around 40 are thought to still be in service today.

In the late 1960s Japan selected the Phantom as its new fighter and also decided to license-produce the aircraft via the Mitsubishi Heavy Industries. The Japan Air Self-Defense Force received a total of 154 F-4EJ and RF-4Es and more than 70 remain in service in 2017.

The Republic of Korea Air Force was supplied with F-4s in the late 1960s, due to on-going tensions with North Korea with the nation receiving 216 F-4Ds, F-4Es and RF-4Cs. Around 70 are still operational in 2017.

McDonnell Douglas F-4 Phantom II production ended in the USA in 1979 and Japan produced its last F-4EJ in May 1981. By that time 5,195 airframes had been built, 5,057 by McDonnell Douglas and 138 under licence in Japan. Of these, 2,874 went to the USAF, 1,264 to the Navy and Marine Corps, and the rest to foreign customers.

The Phantom has seen limited civilian use – with NASA operating the type and a single, privately owned F-4D flown as a 'warbird' in the USA by the Collings Foundation.

Here in the UK Hawker Hunter Aviation at RAF Scampton, Lincolnshire has plans to operate a former Luftwaffe F-4F on defence work should a contract materialise. Although British Phantoms have been absent now for a quarter of a century, 'Phantom Phanatics' have hope that an example may yet grace UK skies once again. ❖

A South Korean F-4E aloft over the region in 1979. Around 70 Phantoms are thought to remain operational with the South Korean Air Force. *USAF*

Whereas the UK built elements of the Phantom under licence, Japan was the only nation to manufacture complete airframes outside the USA. The aircraft remain an integral part of the Japan Air Self-Defense Force in 2017. *US Navy*

The Phantom has served with the air forces of many countries, including Australia, Egypt, Germany, Great Britain, Greece, Iran, Israel, Japan, Spain, South Korea and Turkey. A total of 5,195 were produced between 1958 and 1991.
KEY Collection

The final Phantoms operated by the US military were QF-4 target drones. In their twilight years a number of these were painted in 'retro' schemes and made occasional appearances at airshows across the USA. The type was finally retired in December 2016. *USAF*

On Her Majesty's Service
British Phantoms

Phantom FG.1 XT857 joined the flight test programme in 1967 and was used for carrier trials aboard the USS *Saratoga*. The aircraft is seen here over St Louis, Missouri in November 1968. *Adrian M Balch Collection*

The Phantom would go on to be one of Britain's most capable strike, attack and air defence aircraft – but in the early days it is was an aeroplane that the British forces really didn't want.

From the outset McDonnell Douglas realised its Phantom had enormous export potential and as early as 1959 the company despatched sales teams to Canada, France and Great Britain in search of large orders.

A number of other nations expressed interest in the type but by the early 1960s Britain's Royal Navy (RN) was arguably the most promising lead. The service's Fleet Air Arm (FAA) was in desperate need of a replacement for its ageing de Havilland Sea Vixen fleet defenders and Supermarine Scimitar attack aircraft while the RAF was also looking for a successor to its Hawker Hunters.

In the late 1950s both air arms had put their faith in Hawker Siddeley Aviation (HSA) to produce an aircraft suitable for both land and sea-based units.

HSA initially proposed a variant of its privately funded Hawker P.1121 fighter, but this was quickly abandoned due to a lack of a political support resulting from the release of the 1957 Defence White Paper by Minister of Defence Duncan Sandys MP.

Undeterred, HSA's chief designer, Sir Sydney Camm entered into discussions with Bristol Aero Engines and the two organisations agreed to jointly investigate the prospects of developing a viable combat-capable vertical take-off and landing (VTOL) fighter aircraft. The resulting P.1127 flew in November 1960 but while financial backing for the Pegasus engine was issued by NATO's Mutual Weapons Development Programme, the British Government was not forthcoming with funding.

HSA opted to go ahead with the P.1127 but the then Chief of the Air Staff, Sir Thomas Pike, decreed that a future RAF variant needed to be simpler and a number of his colleagues would only advocate a supersonic aeroplane as the next generation of fighter. Camm actually agreed with this principle and also realised that a supersonic VTOL aircraft would likely be more attractive to potential export customers.

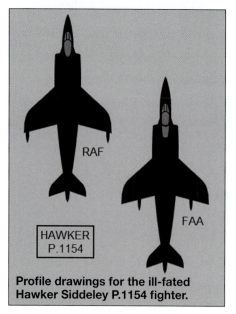

Profile drawings for the ill-fated Hawker Siddeley P.1154 fighter.

The development of the P.1154 was hampered by the need to develop an aeroplane that met both Navy and Air Force needs.

Left: In April 1966 an order was announced for up to 50 F-111Ks and the first two aircraft were in the final stages of assembly when the British Government decided to cancel the project. **Right:** The first British Phantom – YF-4K XT595 – is rolled out of the McDonnell Douglas factory in June 1966. *Boeing*

Supersonic VTOL

Consequently, in April 1961 HSA's board approved preliminary work on a supersonic derivative of the P.1127. Work under the guidance of Ralph Hooper resulted in a new design, designated P.1154. This was 50% larger than the P.1127 and also promised improved performance thanks to 'plenum chamber burning' (afterburning) in the Bristol Siddeley BS100 engine. The engine was equipped with a system of four swivelling exhaust nozzles, similar to the Pegasus used on the P.1127. However, only the front nozzles were to be equipped with chamber burning.

However, by June 1961 the McDonnell Douglas sales team was already actively promoting the Phantom as an alternative. A new F-4B variant even stopped off at RNAS Yeovilton, Somerset on the way back from the Paris Air Salon and the FAA was told the aircraft was available for immediately delivery at a price cheaper than the unproven (and un-flown) P.1154.

The HSA design was finalised and on December 6, 1961 it was decided that the P.1154 would be developed to meet the requirements of both the RAF and the FAA. The type was also pitched to NATO, which had issued a requirement for a VTOL strike fighter, but when that entire programme was shelved HSA was relieved when the Royal Navy's Admiralty and the Ministry of Defence (MoD) both greeted the concept with great interest. Consequently, a first draft of a new joint Naval/Air Staff requirement was issued in the form of Specification OR356/AW406 in April 1962.

As was to be expected the RAF and FAA had different needs and sought very different characteristics in their aircraft. The Air Force wanted a single-seat fighter and interceptor whereas the Navy was looking for a two-seat interceptor capable of low-level strike missions. HSA therefore designed two distinct variants of the P.1154 aircraft, each aimed towards a particular service. Both versions would be armed with the latest Red Top missile.

Although HSA proposed a machine with a tandem undercarriage the Navy pointed out that this was incompatible with the catapults fitted to the era's aircraft carriers; a decision was therefore made to stick with a conventional tricycle undercarriage.

In November 1962, Rolls-Royce offered an alternative power supply to the BS100 in the form of a pair of plenum chamber burning-equipped vectored thrust versions of its Spey engine. The engine manufacturer claimed this powerplant could be available sooner than the BS100, however, many felt the Spey system was inferior, particularly due to the danger posed by asymmetric thrust if one of the two engines failed.

Stillborn Projects

In February 1963 the Minister of Aviation, Julian Amery MP, announced that an order for 600 aircraft (400 for the RAF and 200 for the FAA) was envisioned. By now HSA was realising that it was becoming increasingly difficult to create one aircraft that suited both air arms – not least because the internal equipment varied dramatically. Nevertheless, in May of that year the Secretary of State for Defence, Peter Thorneycroft MP, rejected the option of having two distinct aircraft and official Specification OR356/AW406 called for a single design to be used by both the RAF and the FAA – albeit with different internal radar.

It soon became obvious that a single aircraft could not be developed to meet the needs of both air arms and the project began to slow. Modifications needed to meet naval requirements also resulted in a considerable weight gain and by August 1963, HSA began to openly express concerns that the changes being made to the aircraft were damaging its export potential. Concurrently, a Navy official declared the P.1154 to be a "second rate interceptor" and the RAF began to bemoan the loss of strike performance.

In the background the RAF was fighting its own battle to try to get the BAC TSR-2 beyond the prototype stage. By the early 1960s RAF officials had been told to look for alternatives, in the event of the type being cancelled and attention turned towards the American-built swing-wing General Dynamics F-111.

Many feel that Thorneycroft's decision to stifle the P.1154 programme had been influenced by the F-111 programme. The FAA had already stated a preference for a variable geometry fighter and the purchase of the F-111 would have met the requirements of both air arms at a significantly lower cost than the HSA proposal.

The RAF did evaluate the F-111 as a cheaper option for the TSR-2's intended strike requirement, although the incoming Labour government denied it planned to cancel the British aircraft.

Meanwhile, in late 1963 the government examined three alternative

The YF-4K lands back after its maiden flight on June 27, 1966 with McDonnell Douglas test pilot Joe Dobronski at the controls. *Boeing*

BRITISH PHANTOMS

◄ Compared to Phantoms operated by the USAF and US Navy the British examples shed their General Electric J79 turbojet engines in favour of the Rolls-Royce Spey turbofan. This resulted in the entire centre section of the fuselage being redesigned to accommodate the fatter and shorter Spey. The engine air inlets also needed to be increased in size by 20% to boost airflow to the turbofan; as demonstrated here on the YF-4K. *Boeing*

The Labour government's decision to cancel the TSR-2 programme left the RAF with no replacement for the Canberra. Initial plans called for the F-111K to fill the capability gap but this was also cancelled. *All Key Publishing unless stated*

XT597 was used for deck trials but also became the first British Phantom delivered to the Aircraft & Armament Experimental Establishment. It reached the resident Naval test Squadron late in 1967.

options for the P.1154 programme; 1) to proceed with an RAF-orientated version while delaying the Naval version; 2) continue the development of a full dual-service model with the minimum number of differences; or 3) completely terminate the project.

In November 1963, the *Sunday Telegraph* publicly announced the cancellation of the bi-service P.1154 had been aborted and almost immediately the Royal Navy expressed their open preference for the Phantom.

The following February the Conservative government announced in the House of Commons that a development contract had been placed for the BS100-powered P.1154 as an RAF strike aircraft. It was also announced that the naval requirement would instead be met by Rolls-Royce Spey-engined Phantoms.

The first BS100 engine runs were conducted on October 30, 1964 but the P.1154 ultimately became a victim of the Harold Wilson's incoming Labour government. In November the government informed the Chief of the Air Staff that the P.1154 and TSR-2 projects would both be cancelled (along with the Hawker Siddeley HS.681 V/STOL transport aircraft).

In April 1966 an order was announced for up to 50 F-111Ks (ten firm orders and 40 options that were firmed up a year later). The first two aircraft (XV884 and XV885) were in the final stages of assembly at General Dynamics' plant at Fort Worth, Texas in early 1968 when the government issued a new policy that would see the majority of British forces stationed East of Suez withdrawn by 1971. At the same time the devaluation of sterling had led to the unit cost of each aircraft rising and it was decided to cancel the F-111K procurement.

RAF Replacement

The cancellation of the P.1154 and TSR-2 left the RAF with no Hunter or Canberra replacement. As it had already been decided that the FAA was to receive the Phantom, it seemed logical that the RAF should do likewise.

The announcement was made by Prime Minister Harold Wilson on February 2, 1965. The RAF's original requirement was for 200 aircraft, but stringent controls on defence spending reduced the number to 116 plus two prototypes. The Labour government authorised the large-scale purchase of American aircraft 'on credit' as replacements (initially to also include the F-111K) and orders were placed for F-4 Phantoms and Lockheed C-130K Hercules – the latter to fill the gap created by the cancellation of the HS.681.

The cost and time savings compared to designing and creating aircraft from scratch was considered worthwhile but the loss of British jobs and export potential would be immense. To placate the ailing aviation industry the government negotiated for British companies to produce up to 40% of each Phantom under licence. In practice this mostly meant producing small items but the British Aircraft Corporation (BAC) at Warton, Lancashire was awarded the contract for producing the F-4 rear fuselages (normally built for McDonnell Douglas by Fairchild), Shorts at Belfast manufactured the outer wing sections and Ferranti licence-produced the AN/AWG-10 radar.

By far the largest change to British Phantoms was also a result of the desire to maintain British jobs. It was decided to change the US-built Phantoms' General Electric J79 turbojet engine in favour of the Rolls-Royce Spey turbofan. On paper this offered a 25% increase in thrust as well as reducing both take-off distances and fuel consumption by a third; however the entire centre section of the fuselage had to be redesigned to accommodate the fatter and shorter

The British Phantom's first public appearance was at the 1968 SBAC Farnborough show. Phantom FG.1 XT859 from the Navy's 700P squadron wowed the crowds in less than ideal weather conditions.
Richard Cousens via Awyr Aviation Communication Ltd

FAA Phantoms had to operate from shorter carrier decks than their US cousins. The nose oleo therefore needed to be extendable so that the aircraft could sit with a much higher angle of attack during take-off in order to reduce the amount of wind needed over the deck at launch. The leg itself was 40in taller than on a 'normal' Phantom.

Whilst based on the F-4K, the RAF's F-4M lacked the naval-variant's lengthened oleo, catapult hooks, slatted tailplane, aileron droop and hinged radar (only the nose-cone was hinged). The first YF-4M was XT852, which flew for the first time on February 17, 1967. *Boeing*

Phantom FGR.2 XT907 visits US Naval Air Station Patuxent River, Maryland in 1970 on detachment. XT907 was one of the breed's lucky survivors and survives today at Bentwaters Airfield in Suffolk. *US Navy*

Spey. The engine air inlets also needed to be increased in size by 20% to boost airflow to the turbofan and titanium had to be used in the aft fuselage to allow for the higher exhaust gas temperatures.

Furthermore, wind tunnel testing showed the vastly redesigned fuselage and engine bay interfered with the drag-reducing 'area rule' contours. The deeper fuselage also caused extra base-drag and these factors combined to negate much of the promised performance increases. However there was at least one advantage – the Speys were significantly less smoky than the J79s, so a British F-4 was much harder to spot during air combat!

Admiralty Phantom

Both the RAF and FAA Phantoms were to be based on the US Navy's F-4J variant. The F-4M would be operated by the RAF whereas the F-4K would be used by the Admiralty.

The F-4K needed to be made compatible with the RN's carriers, which were much smaller than those used by the US Navy – both in terms of storage space and the length of deck available to take-off and land upon.

In order to fit on the deck lifts the F-4K was modified to enable the entire nose radome and radar to fold through 180 degrees. The nose leg also needed to be extendable so that the aircraft could sit with a much higher angle of attack at take-off in order to reduce the amount of wind needed over the deck at launch. The leg itself was 40in (1.02m) taller than on a 'normal' Phantom. Larger flaps, drooping ailerons and slatted tailplanes were also added to improve slow speed performance and the main undercarriage and arrestor hook were strengthened to allow landings at both higher sink speeds and weights.

All of the work took so much money and time that the supposedly cheap 'off-the-shelf' order turned into a protracted and expensive procurement. Whilst a laudable policy, the outcome of 'anglicising' the Phantom was an aircraft some three times the flyaway the price of the US Navy's F-4J and – as time would tell – having a poorer performance in most areas.

The F-4M airframes destined for the RAF did not need such modifications. In fact the RAF would have been content with a standard F-4 and even viewed the change to Spey engines as completely unnecessary. As they correctly surmised, the changes consumed up valuable time and money that could have been used to finance extra aircraft.

Maiden Flight

The first British Phantom to fly was the YF-4K (XT595), which took to the skies on June 27, 1966 with McDonnell Douglas test pilot Joe Dobronski at the controls.

Testing showed the Spey-engined machine had less fuel consumption and greater acceleration at low altitude but as the aircraft climbed the performance fell away and soon became inferior to the F-4J. Problems included slow throttle response and erratic burner light up above 45,000ft. The F-4K was also only capable of flying at Mach 1.9 compared to the F-4J's top speed of Mach 2.1.

Changes were therefore required to the engine/intake/jet nozzle configurations and this pushed back the proposed entry to service date by almost two years.

In the meantime, XT596 joined the flight test programme in 1967 while XT857 and XT597 began carrier trials aboard the USS *Saratoga* two years later.

XT597 would also be the first British Phantom delivered to the Aircraft & Armament Experimental Establishment (A&AEE) at Boscome Down, Wiltshire. It reached the resident Naval test Squadron late in 1967 and on April 30, 1968 the Navy's 700P Naval Air Squadron (NAS) was formed at RNAS Yeovilton to conduct fleet trials.

The British Phantom's first public

BRITISH PHANTOMS

Initial training of RAF Phantom crews was undertaken by 228 OCU at RAF Coningsby. XT901 joined the squadron in October 1968 and flew with the RAF until it was finally scrapped in 1991.

Air-to-air refuelling techniques were also delegated to the squadron to teach. Here a Phantom FG.1 from 43 Sqn approaches a USAF KC-135 Stratotanker of the 306th Strategic Refuelling Wing on September 1, 1980. *USAF*

Left: In air defence 'fit' the Phantom could carry four AIM-7E Sparrow III or BAe Skyflash and four AIM-9D/L Sidewinder air-to-air missiles. **Right:** This quartet of 43 Sqn Phantoms consists of (from front to back) XV571, XT874, XV583 and XV575. All four survived until the 1990s when the Phantom fleet was retired and were scrapped at either Leuchars or Wattisham

appearance was made by a 700P example at the 1968 SBAC show at Farnborough – where the Spey-powered goliath certainly made an impression on the crowd! [Ed: the service career of the Royal Navy's Phantoms is discussed in more detail on p28]

Unenthusiastic Start

While the Admiralty was seemingly delighted with their new aircraft the Phantom met with a less enthusiastic reception at the RAF. Air force personnel often felt they had been left with no option but to operate the big 'Navy' fighter and had been forced to sacrifice their preferred P.1154 due to Navy meddling in the project. Nevertheless, they had little choice in the matter and were forced to make the best of an aircraft they did not want, did not believe in and felt was compromised to make it suitable for both RAF and FAA operations.

Whilst based on the F-4K, the RAF's F-4M lacked the naval-variant's lengthened oleo, catapult hooks, slatted tailplane, aileron droop and hinged radar (only the nose-cone was hinged).

The Phantom was to be designated the FGR.2 in RAF service – referring to the aircraft's role as an air-defence fighter, ground attack strike aircraft and tactical reconnaissance machine. Although it generally only needed to fulfil one of these functions at any given time the F-4M's diverse capabilities required a more specialised equipment fit than its Naval cousin. An Inertial Navigation & Attack System (INAS) was produced by Ferranti and based upon the unit the RAF had specified for the ill-fated TSR-2. This operated alongside an AD470 HF radio that allowed over-the-horizon communication on low-level sorties and an EMI-designed reconnaissance pod – the latter housing up to five optical film cameras, infra-red linescan and sideways-looking airborne radar. It also had mapping and moving target indication capabilities.

Other changes included the addition of anti-skid brakes, provision for a centre-line mounted SUU-23 gun pod and a complete revision of its avionics. Combined, these changes meant that 45% of F-4Ms were produced in the UK, compared to 40% of the Navy's F-4K.

The first Phantom produced for the RAF was YF-4M XT852, which flew for the first time on February 17, 1967. Like the YF-4K this aircraft also suffered from powerplant issues which delayed its eventual delivery, but further hold-ups were caused by interfacing problems between the INAS and the AN/AWG 12 radar. By the time the problems had been sorted XV406 and XV410 had already entered service in the UK, trialling the recce pod and HF radio respectively.

RAF Service

Delivery of production FGR.2s began in July 1968 and by October the following year, the RAF's last Phantom had been received. All RAF aircraft were flown first to 23 Maintenance Unit (MU) at RAF Aldergrove, Northern Ireland prior to acceptance. Training for RAF Phantom crews was carried out by 228 Operational Conversion Unit (OCU) at RAF Coningsby, Lincolnshire, which received its first aircraft on August 23, 1968.

Initially the OCU was tasked with training crews for 6 Sqn, which formed at RAF Coningsby, Lincolnshire on January 13, 1969. The squadron was officially established on May 7, taking on the primary operational duties of ground attack and tactical support.

The next Phantom unit was 54 Sqn, which formed on September 1, 1969, at Coningsby, where it operated in the ground attack role until being disbanded on April 22, 1974.

Both 6 and 54 Sqns were tasked with supporting NATO forces around the globe and were often deployed overseas. For example, during the Turkish invasion of northern Cyprus in August 1974, Phantoms from 6 Sqn was deployed to RAF Akrotiri, Cyprus to provide air support to UN forces on the island. Shortly after its return to the UK the squadron was disbanded on September

A pair of 111 Sqn Phantom FGR.2s pose for the camera in the early 1970s with XV416 in the foreground and XV414 behind. On March 3, 1975 XV416 crashed into the River Witham shortly after take-off from RAF Coningsby following engine failure. Luckily both crew ejected safely. Five years later, on December 12, 1980, the crew XV414 were also forced to eject – this time after a fuel leak ignited. The jet crashed into the North Sea two miles off Great Yarmouth, Norfolk.

30, 1974. The third Coningsby Phantom unit was 41 Sqn, which formed there on April 1, 1972 and provided dedicated tactical reconnaissance until March 31, 1977, when it disbanded.

Unlike its sister units at Coningsby, 29 Sqn was tasked with UK air defence, taking over the role from the English Electric Lightning. It was formed on October 1, 1974 and achieved operational status the following May.

Although the F-4K had been designed for the FAA – and was flown by the Navy as the FG.1 – a total of 20 aircraft from the original RN order were flown directly to 23 MU for modification. These aircraft had originally been destined to operate from HMS *Eagle* but the cancellation of the ship's planned refit meant they would be delivered to 43 Sqn at RAF Leuchars, Fife.

The squadron was formed on September 1, 1969 and declared operational on July 1, 1970, with the dual role of UK air defence and tactical air support of maritime operations. As the FG.1's weapon systems was already optimised for air defence, they were ideally suited for 43 Sqn's role of quick reaction alert (QRA) as they did not need to wait for the lengthy process of aligning the inertial platform before taxiing.

During this period of the Cold War the most likely threats were low flying interdiction aircraft such as the Sukhoi Su-24 *Fencer*, a scenario in which the Phantom excelled. However, following a change in NATO's defence policy in 1972 to the so-called 'flexible response', Phantoms took over high altitude air defence tasks from the less capable English Electric Lightnings at Leuchars and RAF Wattisham, Suffolk. As had been demonstrated during the trials programme the Phantom's real weakness was its performance degradation at high altitude, but it was the best aircraft available at the time.

The Northern UK Air Defence Region (UKADR) was officially formed at Coningsby on October 1, 1974 with cover being provided by Phantom FGR.2s from 43 Sqn and 111 Sqn. The Northern UKADR moved to Leuchars in November 3, 1975, where it later re-equipped with FG.1s.

Phantoms from Leuchars were better suited to long-range interceptions over the North Sea than the then-prevalent Lightnings, and 43 Sqn's aircraft were soon regularly intercepting Soviet intruders.

Control of the Southern UKADR was mainly shared between the two Lightning squadrons at RAF Binbrook, Lincolnshire, and three Phantom units at Wattisham. The first of the units to form at Wattisham was 23 Sqn, which arrived on February 25, 1976. The unit remained at the base until 1983 when it was relocated to the Falkland Islands [Ed: see p78].

The late 1970s saw the withdrawal of the FAA's last Phantoms. With HMS *Ark Royal* sent to the scrapyard in 1978 there was no ship from which to operate and the Navy was now reliant on the RAF for air defence of the fleet.

The *Ark*'s Phantom FG.1s from 892 NAS were flown to Leuchars and handed over to the RAF's 111 Sqn, which in turn passed its FGR.2s onto other squadrons.

Left: In its air defence role, the Phantom's principal peacetime task was to hold Quick Reaction Alert, which it did from numerous fighter stations. In the UK, Phantoms held ten-minute readiness with the effort being split between Northern and Southern QRA. *PRMAVIA Collection* **Right:** FG.1 XT875 powers into the sky at RAF Chivenor in August 1970. This airframe served until 1991 and was ultimately scrapped at RAF Wattisham, Suffolk. *Adrian M Balch*

BRITISH PHANTOMS

Left: Ex-Fleet Air Arm FG.1s proved ideal for 43 Sqn's Quick Reaction Alert role. Their weapon systems were already optimised for air defence and they did not need to wait for the lengthy process of aligning the inertial platform before taxiing. Here, XV574 intercepts a Soviet Tupolev Tu-95 *Bear* bomber over the North Sea. **Right:** Phantom FGR.2 XV401 on detachment to Luqa, Malta in 1974 while in service with 41 Sqn. *Airspace Images*

Left: A quartet of 43 Sqn Phantoms perform at an airshow at RAF Leuchars in the early 1970s. *Airspace Images*
Right: With the eventual 'cooling' of the Cold War the Phantom fleet spent more of its time on air defence duties and less emphasis was placed on ground attack/strike work. As such, the aircraft's camouflage was changed to low visibility grey.

RAF Germany

Although it had got off to an inauspicious start the RAF Phantom fleet was to find an enthusiastic home in Europe. The type equipped six front-line squadrons in RAF Germany (RAFG) at a time when it formed the front line of the Cold War.

Phantoms initially replaced Canberras and Hunters in the strike/attack and reconnaissance roles and the first RAFG unit was 14 Sqn, which formed at RAF Brüggen on July 1, 1970. The base was also home to 17 Sqn from September 1, 1970 and 31 Sqn from July 20, 1971 – the latter having a secondary reconnaissance role.

Brüggen's Phantoms operated in the nuclear strike role and were armed with the US Mk.57 low-yield nuclear store. This was fitted with a retard parachute to allow free-fall, loft, or retard methods of delivery.

The first dedicated Phantom reconnaissance unit was 2 Sqn, which formed at Brüggen on December 1, 1970 and moved to its operational base at RAF Laarbruch on May 3 of the following year. In due course all of the RAFG strike/attack Phantoms were replaced by SEPECAT Jaguars, with 14 Sqn being the first unit to be re-equipped (on November 30, 1975). With the build up of the Jaguar force in the strike/attack role, Phantoms were released to take over air defence tasks from the Lightnings serving with RAFG. Two units were based at RAF Wildenrath with 19 Sqn arriving on October 1, 1976 and 92 Sqn joining it on April 1, 1977.

In the air defence role the RAFG Phantom's standard weapons fit was four AIM-7 Sparrow or Skyflash medium-range air-to-air missiles, plus four AIM-9L Sidewinders on twin-launchers on the inner-wing pylons. Additionally, a SUU-23/A gun pod was carried on the centreline pylon and two drop tanks were carried on the outer pylons.

For a large aeroplane the Phantom was certainly no slouch!

Additional Order

The deployment of 23 Sqn to the Falkland Islands in 1983, combined with attrition and airframe fatigue led to a shortage of Phantoms capable of providing cover for the UKADR force. Delays in the Tornado ADV programme potentially left a gaping hole in the UK's air defence capabilities so the British Government purchased 15 surplus US Navy F-4Js as a stopgap measure. These were refurbished and designated as the F-4J(UK) with the first being declared operational with 74 Sqn at Wattisham on October 19, 1984.

Compared to their F-4K and F-4M counterparts the aircraft featured brand new J79-GE-10B engines. Unlike some of the earlier F-4J variants, the engines for the F-4J(UK) airframes were modified to eliminate smoke emission. Although the J79 was not as powerful as the Spey it had instantaneous power response and handled better at higher altitudes.

Compared to other RAF Phantoms the F-4J(UK)s were easy to spot by virtue of their slimmer fuselages and, initially, blue/grey scheme that was applied over yellow primer and gave the aircraft a turquoise hue in certain lights. Eventually the aircraft were repainted into the standard air defence grey.

As significant as the change of engines was the more fundamental difference to earlier British airframes was the more modern missile control system. Based

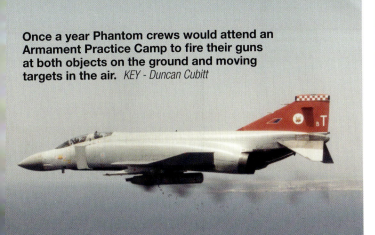

Once a year Phantom crews would attend an Armament Practice Camp to fire their guns at both objects on the ground and moving targets in the air. *KEY - Duncan Cubitt*

Phantom FGR.2 XV433 stays low on take-off from RAF Akrotiri in Cyprus in 1991.

Left: When they were delivered the F-4J(UK)s were easy to spot compared to the FGR.2s. As well as their slimmer fuselages they were painted in a blue/grey scheme that was applied over yellow primer and gave the aircraft a turquoise hue in certain lights. **Right:** The British Phantom's real weakness was its performance degradation at high altitude, but the Spey-engined aircraft was the best the UK had available at the time.

For many years the Phantom force maintained 24/7 QRA duties, scrambling at a moments notice come day or night.

Phantoms from 56 Sqn and 74 Sqn await their next sortie. The RAF operated a large fleet of the type from 1968 until 1992.

upon the Westinghouse AWG-10 pulse-Doppler radar, it was equivalent to the Grumman F-14 Tomcat weapon system technology.

Other changes included more ergonomically designed cockpits (complete with a combined ejection system that could be commanded from the front seat), a radar warning antennae on the air intake sides and internal chaff and flare dispensers. The variant could also carry a centre-line fuel tank without incurring a 'G' restriction. (In fitting Speys to the FG.1s/FGR.2s, the tank support area structure was weakened, thus reducing the maximum 'G' limit.)

When the first heavily modified Phantoms were ordered for British forces in the 1960s nobody could have predicted that the best-performing RAF air defence Phantom would prove to be a 'stock' F-4J variant!

Likewise, nobody could have predicted that the F-4M would ultimately cost twice

as much as 'standard' F-4D version. The programme would also eventually exceed the overall cost of the P.1154 project and the politically motivated decision to alter the airframe and build elements of it under licence would result in a £100 million development cost and make the British

◀ **The Spey-engined FGR.2 and FG.1 had less fuel consumption and greater acceleration at low altitude than the F-4J. Although it was less smoky than the J79 powered variants its still left a tell tale streak in the sky at certain power settings.**

F-4s the most expensive of all Phantoms ever produced! Throughout their lives UK Phantoms were to receive over 1,000 modifications, many to overcome fatigue problems associated with operating the aircraft at low-level.

Ultimately, the British Government would receive 52 F-4K/FG.1 airframes, 118 F-4M/FGR.2s and 15 F-4J(UK) airframes but in UK service the Phantom would never fire its guns in anger. However, it provided vital air defence and strike/attack capability for the UK, Germany and the Falkland Islands. It also developed a fond following from pilots, ground crew and enthusiasts alike and earned legendary status in the aviation world. ➡

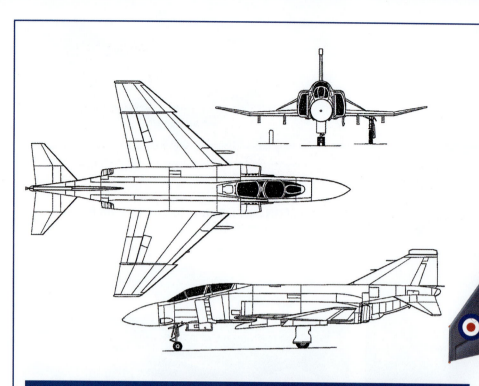

SPECIFICATION

McDonnell Douglas F-4K (FG.1) & F-4M (FGR.2) Phantom II

Crew	2
Length	57ft 11in (17.65m)
Height	16ft 5in (5.00m)
Wingspan	38ft 5in (11.71m)
Wingspan (folded)	27ft 7in (8.41m)
Wing area	530sq ft (49.2m^2)
Empty Weight	30,000lb (13,608kg)
Loaded Weight	49,000lb (22,226kg)
Max Take-Off Weight	58,000lb (26,309kg)
Max Speed	1,090kts (Mach 1.9/1,255mph/2,020km/h) at 36,000ft 790kts (Mach 1.2/909mph/1,463km/h) at 1,000ft
Service Ceiling	60,000ft (18,300m)
Ferry Range	2,500 miles (4,024km)
Tactical Radius	550 miles (885km)
Powerplant	Two Rolls-Royce RB.165-25R Spey Mk.202/203 afterburning turbofans (22,550lb/thrust each with reheat)
Armament (Air Defence)	One 20mm M61A1 Vulcan rotary cannon in centreline pod, four AIM-7E Sparrow III or BAe Skyflash and four AIM-9D/L Sidewinder air-to-air missiles.
Armament (Strike)	Various external ordinance including eleven 1,000lb Mk.14 bombs, ten Matra pods (each with 18 x 68mm rockets) and Martel air-to-surface missiles.
First Flight	June 27, 1966 (YF-4K) February 17, 1967 (YF-4M)

Above and above right:
McDonnell Douglas F-4K Phantom FG.1 XT864 first flew on April 4, 1968 and was delivered to the Admiralty on July 17 of the same year. It is seen here wearing the markings of 892 NAS but also flew with 767 NAS and 700P with the Fleet Air Arm and 111 Sqn with the RAF at Leuchars, Fife. The aircraft was badly damaged on December 6, 1988 when the tailplane was "forcibly removed by a fuel bowser." With the withdrawal of the type it was not repaired and was allocated to 8998M and placed on the gate at Leuchars. When the base closed the aircraft was disposed of and transferred to the Ulster Aviation Society collection at Long Kesh. *Key Publishing/Pete West*

▼ McDonnell Douglas F-4K Phantom FG.1 XT864 performed its maiden flight on April 9, 1968 and joined the Fleet Air Arm on July 1. It flew with 892 NAS, 767 NAS (illustrated) and 700P before joining the RAF and flying with 43 Sqn and 111 Sqn. It retired in 1989 and was scrapped at RAF Abingdon, Oxfordshire. *Key Publishing/Pete West*

McDonnell Douglas F-4K Phantom FG.1 XV574 in the markings of 43 Sqn. The aircraft was delivered to the RAF on February 14, 1969 and also flew with 111 Sqn, with whom it gained a special scheme just prior to being scrapped in 1991 [see page 36]. *Andy Hay/www.flyingart.co.uk*

McDonnell Douglas F-4K Phantom FG.1 XV571 in the air defence grey markings it wore with 43 Sqn. The aircraft had first flown on November 12, 1968 and joined the RAF the following June. It spent its entire career with 43 Sqn and 111 Sqn before being scrapped at RAF Leuchars, Fife in April 1992 *Key Publishing/Pete West*

Flying the Phantom

F-4 from the Cockpit

The Phantom was a large aeroplane that boasted a maximum take-off weight in the region of 58,000lbs, yet it proved capable in the interceptor and ground attack roles.

Air Commodore Rick Peacock-Edwards CBE AFC FRAeS FCIM flew the English Electric Lightning, McDonnell Douglas F-4 Phantom and Panavia Tornado F.2/F.3 during a stellar RAF career. He explains to Steve Bridgewater why the Phantom was a real war machine.

The son of a Battle of Britain pilot, Rick Peacock-Edwards was educated in South Africa from where he joined the RAF in 1965. He spent over 30 years in the RAF and retired as an Air Commodore in 1999 with a number of achievements under his belt, including Station Commander at RAF Leeming, Deputy Commander RAF Staff Washington, Inspector of Flight Safety and Director of Eurofighter.

His flying career has been spent mainly on fighters and he has over 1,000 hours on each of the Lightning, Phantom and Tornado. He also has over 1,000 hours on the Folland Gnat and has flown many other types including the BAe Hawk and Hawker Hunter.

Rick's introduction to the Phantom came in 1977 and followed his second Lightning tour (as an instructor on 65 Sqn at the RAF Coltishall OCU) and a brief tour instructing on both the Gnat and Hunter at RAF Valley.

"Although I had more than 1,000 hours on the Lightning my return to the air defence world was something of a culture shock" Rick reveals. "You see, my operational fighter flying to date had been purely in single-seaters – and now I had to get used to the concept of sharing the cockpit and operating as part of a two-crew team."

Training Aids

"My pilot training intake was supposed to be a 'short course' as we were all ex-Lightning chaps," continues Rick, "but as they had a bunch of 'baby navigators' they asked us if we'd mind doing the 'long course' instead. So that's what we did.

"We all came together as a class – pilots and navigators alike – at the start of the course and we worked together from day one. Of course there were some parts of the syllabus that the navigators did separately but most of the time we were working together."

Flight training had also come along leaps and bounds in the few short years since Rick had converted onto the Lightning. "My abiding memory of the Phantom course was that we didn't fly anywhere near as much as we had done when we learned to fly the Lightning," he says. "By now the training aids were far more advanced than we had had access to on the Lightning so much more training was undertaken on the ground in the simulator or using airborne intercept training aids."

It also took longer to prepare the Phantom for each training flight. "The preparation for every sortie in the F-4 took a lot longer than the Lightning,"

The cockpit of the Phantom was distinctly '60s in design and feel. The front cockpit was roomy with the aircraft designed to be flown right-handed. A pedestal-mounted control column in the centre was fitted with a complex stick top which contained a trim switch, stores release button, nosewheel steering button and a trigger. Dominating the forward view was the radar repeater display and the lead computing optical sighting system *Dave Gledhill*

Rick explains. "Of course this was partly because of the aircraft's more complex systems and advanced weapons but we also had the added element of a second crewmember, so briefings just took longer. In fact, a standard briefing on the Phantom course took at least 45 minutes."

That said, the big American-designed fighter could carry far more fuel than the Lightning so the average missions were also of greater endurance. Consequently, the subsequent debrief therefore took longer as well.

This was quite a shock to the ex-Lightning pilots on the course. "When we learned to fly the Lightning we would sometimes fly two or three sorties a day," says Rick, "whereas with the Phantom we were lucky to fly two or three times a week."

War Machine

Like all of his contemporaries Rick was an enormous fan of the Lightning. "It was fantastic fun to fly," he says, but the aircraft had its shortcomings. It was lacking in both range and armament and you had to be able to keep pace with the sheer speed of operations. However,

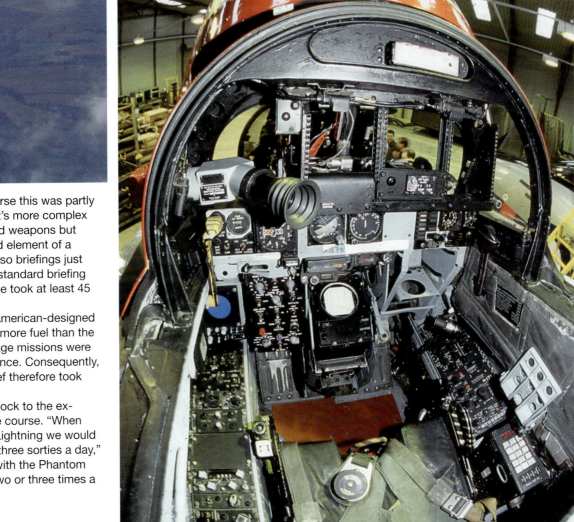

The rear cockpit was fondly described as the 'ergonomic slum'. Seemingly an afterthought, the main equipment was hidden away in 'cubby holes' and only pulled out in the air. The main radar controls were across the front bulkhead and comprised a display unit – the scope – topped by a radar film camera assembly, a navigator's hand control on the right and the main radar control panel by the left knee

PHANTOM | 23

FROM THE COCKPIT

Rick intercepted around 30 Tupolev *Bear* and *Badger* bombers during his RAF career.

The Phantom was really powerful at low-level and had a greater G limit than the Lightning. *All KEY Collection unless stated*

Rick Peacock-Edwards flew the Lightning, Phantom and Tornado operationally with the RAF and instructed on the Gnat and Hunter. He was also Assistant Air Attache in Washington, Inspector of Flight Safety for the RAF and Director of Eurofighter Typhoon. In his post RAF career he has been Director of Government Affairs at General Dynamics UK, Managing Director of Vector Flying Training Services and has consulted for a number of UK companies. He is a Past Master of the Honourable Company of Air Pilots, President of the Historic Aircraft Association and Chairman of the General Aviation Safety Council (GASCo), the International Air Cadets Training organisation, the Aviation Focus Group and the Imperial War Museum Duxford Flying Control Committee and Vice Chairman of the prestigious Royal Air Force Club in London. Rick is currently the Chief Operating Officer at In Command Ltd.

the F-4 was a new generation of fighter. "The Phantom was a real war machine," Rick extols. "You felt very comfortable in its capabilities. For the time it was a real improvement compared to the Lightning, just as the Tornado was a real improvement over the Phantom a generation later.

"The radar was much more capable, you had an Inertial Navigation System [INS], you had a greater choice of weapons – and more of them – in fact everything was just more advanced."

The progression through the flying training syllabus began with student pilots flying from the front cockpit with a Qualified Flying Instructor (QFI) taking the place of the navigator in the rear seat.

Meanwhile, the trainee navigators had been busy using the various simulators and classroom aids before they received their first flights in back of jets flown by experienced pilots.

"Once you were deemed ready you were ultimately sent off on your first 'crew' solo," Rick explains. "This would be the first time the 'new' pilot would fly with a 'new' navigator. The entire training syllabus then built steadily as the days went on moving on from general handling sorties to night flying and formation work. In my case the entire course took just under six months and I then moved on to 111 Sqn (Tremblers) at RAF Leuchars in August 1977."

OCU Flying

At the conclusion of the initial conversion training the new Phantom crews continued their training on the OCU by advancing to the more operational and tactical parts of the course. "Here we would start to receive basic weapons training before building up our intercept skills and tactics," says Rick. "Then we'd move onto the advanced weapons course, which included intercepts with a lot of 'evasion'. The capabilities of

A Phantom uses its braking parachute to slow down at the end of a sortie.

At high altitude the Phantom's Rolls-Royce Spey turbofans began to lose power, and performance fell off the higher the aircraft got.

"Start One." The crew of a 56 Sqn Phantom signal to the groundcrew ahead of spooling up the Phantom's Spey engines.

Phantom's missiles meant you also practised for both front hemisphere and rear hemisphere attacks. Again, the OCU course was a cumulative syllabus and each sortie saw us flying more and learning new things."

The next stage in the rookie Phantom crew's training involved more extensive combat simulations. "We began fighting another Phantom crew as part of a 'one vs one' sortie and then progressed via 'two vs one' to 'two vs two', constantly honing our air combat manoeuvring skills."

In order to graduate from the OCU each crew would need to employ all the skills they had learned on the basic and advanced courses – as well as the OCU – as part of a simulated 'final course sortie' wartime scenario.

"The entire sortie would be assessed," Rick explains, "from the briefing throughout to our airmanship, tactics, success rate and ultimately how we conducted the final debrief back in the crew room."

> ## "The 'opposing' crew would have been briefed to make our intercept as difficult as possible"

"I was assigned to an air defence squadron so in my case the scenario could have involved intercepting either a slow moving aeroplane such as a Cessna or a fast moving bomber/fighter or a high flying bomber.. That intercept could take place at ultra-low-level, very high altitude or anywhere in between. Furthermore, the 'opposing' crew would have been briefed to make our intercept as difficult as possible. Of course, you could expect to be 'bounced' by another aircraft along the way, forcing you to put your defensive skills to the test as well."

Assuming everything went to plan, the pilot and navigator would then get a 'tick in the box' and be sent off to an operational squadron as a newly graduated crew.

Multi-Crew

The squadron crew room was a very different environment from that which Rick was used to – and there were far more people involved at every level. "That took some getting used to," Rick admits. "On a Lightning unit there were generally 12 aircraft and around 15 pilots – you were a little 'Band of Brothers'. Suddenly we now found ourselves with twice as many people, but it soon became obvious that the capabilities of the aircraft and its crew far outshone its predecessor."

XV568 first flew on April 29, 1968 and was delivered to the RAF in July of the same year. It survived until the end of the Phantom's career and was ultimately scrapped at RAF Leuchars in 1992.

Left: A Phantom stands ready for launch. The aircraft served the RAF for almost 25 years and earned the respect of those who flew it or worked on it. **Right:** Even at squadron level the training regime continued unabated. These crews examine the target towed by a 100 Sqn Canberra for live fire practice during a detachment to Cyprus.

"A two-crew aircraft that works together well as a team is far more effective than a single-seater," Rick continues. "But for that to happen the crew needs to work together – otherwise it can be a disaster. Therefore, an important part of the training course is what would nowadays be referred to as Crew Resource Management. This instilled in us the best ways to communicate and work efficiently as part of a team.

"My regular navigator was a 'first tourist' and a really lovely guy but I remember one sortie in particular that emphasised the need for good crew communication. On that occasion we were in a multi-aircraft formation and were pretty much upside down when he called "check fuel".... I had to explain that I was a little bit busy at the time!

"In fact, all the navigators I flew with during my career were superb and a real pleasure to fly with."

Recalling another incident that caught his attention, Rick remembers: "I had three tanks on and I'd been leading a pair of Phantoms from Leuchars at night; we'd been up on a night tanker, so I was absolutely full of fuel when my number two went unserviceable and went back to Leuchars.

"So there I was with a heavy aircraft, full of fuel and time on my hands, so I went on a practice diversion to Lossiemouth. This was about eleven o'clock at night. I was too heavy to put the wheels on the ground, but as I came into the overshoot there was an almighty bang and the whole sky lit up, and traffic control said: 'You're on fire, you're on fire.'

"I looked out and I wasn't on fire – but one of my engines had blown up and had just seized solid. The fire that they saw was actually bits of blades coming out of the back end. In fact they picked up a bag of them, afterwards! With the Phantom you need reheat to climb on one engine, so if the good engine hadn't lit, I'd have been in a possible eject situation. Fortunately the reheat on the good engine did light and I was able to climb away. My navigator in the back seat said: 'What's going on?' (or words to that effect!) but once again I was too busy to explain at that very moment!"

Ten Bear Club

During his time with 111 Sqn at RAF Leuchars Rick was regularly launched as part of the Quick Reaction Alert (QRA) network of air defence fighters.

"We got scrambled a lot to intercept the Russian *Bears* and *Badgers*," he explains, "so I've seen plenty of those. And I'm a member of the '*Ten Bear Club*' – when you've intercepted ten *Bears*, you get a badge with a bear on it. I've probably intercepted about 30 *Badgers*, *Bears*, day and night, and very interesting it was too. I remember I had a pair of *Badgers* one time, which I intercepted about three in the morning – they did some fairly sporty manoeuvring whilst I was in behind them.

"They were on a variety of missions – sometimes it would just be a transit flight to Cuba; sometimes they would be exercising with the Russian Navy in the North Atlantic – they had a war mission that they would practise. And sometimes they went down into the oil fields of the North Sea, but of course it's international waters to within 12 miles of the coast. We would get airborne, link up with the tanker, intercept the *Bears*

Left: A pair of 74 Sqn Phantoms at medium altitude. XT910 was scrapped at RAF Shawbury in 1995 whereas XV460 was retired to decoy duties at RAF Coningsby. It eventually met the scrapman's axe but the nose has been saved for posterity.
Right: Live ammunition is loaded for the Phantom's M61A1 Vulcan rotary cannon during an armament training camp in Cyprus.

Left: The Phantom was at its best at high speed and low-level. **Right:** The genesis of British supersonic interceptors from Lightning (top) through Phantom to Tornado F.3 (bottom). All three were flown operationally by the Rick Peacock-Edwards.

and *Badgers* and shadow them. Sometimes that was at medium level; sometimes at low level.

"We'd photograph them, and they'd photograph us. We'd know they were coming long before we'd intercept them as we worked in conjunction with the RAF Shackletons and the American AWACS aircraft. It was very much a co-ordinated operation. Most of the Russian aircraft would come around what we call the North Cape, so the Norwegian radar would see them and we'd know they were coming. The Americans were based in Keflavik, in Iceland, with F-15s and AWACS, so whether it was Norwegian F-16s or F-15s from America, or us with the Phantoms, it was always a very co-ordinated exercise – NATO working together.

"We had an area of responsibility, which was called the United Kingdom Air Defence Region, so when they were in our region, that was our responsibility. It's a big bit of sky."

Idiosyncrasies

"I'm yet to fly an aircraft I didn't like" admits Rick, but he is fond of all the aircraft that he has flown including the big Phantom.

"I enjoyed flying the Phantom greatly but it was very different to the Lightning that went before it and the Tornado that followed it into service. It did have some interesting little characteristics and idiosyncrasies, for example when the Phantom was turning tightly and loaded up with 'G' – somewhere above 16 units of angle-of-attack (AoA) – you could not fly the aeroplane with ailerons. It suffered from adverse raw and the ailerons actually turned you the opposite direction – so you had to use rudder to turn at high G.

"In my opinion the Phantom was the easiest jet fighter to land. As it had originally been designed for aircraft carrier operations you didn't need to 'kick off' drift or flare – you just flew it onto the runway and it sorted itself out!

"All in all, the Phantom was a nice aeroplane to fly – it was just a little different to the Lightning I was used to. It was really powerful at low level and had a greater G limit than the Lightning but it wasn't as good at high altitude as the Speys ran out of 'puff' the higher they got. In my opinion that was the Phantom's only real disappointment.

"Like every aeroplane I've flown, the Phantom became a completely different machine when it broke through the sound barrier. It was like a thoroughbred racehorse – it liked to go fast and it went fast really well."

Rick flew the Phantom from 1977 until 1980 when he then progressed to his first tour at the MOD followed by attendance at the RAF Staff College at Bracknell from where he was selected to be the first RAF pilot to convert to the new Panavia Tornado F.2 and command the first squadron (229 OCU/65 Sqn).

"As it happened, there was a slight delay in the Tornado programme which meant I had the opportunity to 'keep my hand in' flying the Phantom. In total I accumulated a total of 1,100 hours – I really enjoyed my flying, in fact I was known as a 'hog'!"

Rick would go on to introduce the Tornado F.2 (and later F.3) into RAF service but retains a strong affinity with the fabulous Phantom. ❖

GREAT SUBSCRIPTION OFFERS FROM

SUBSCRIBE
TO *YOUR* FAVOURITE MAGAZINE
AND SAVE
Phantom

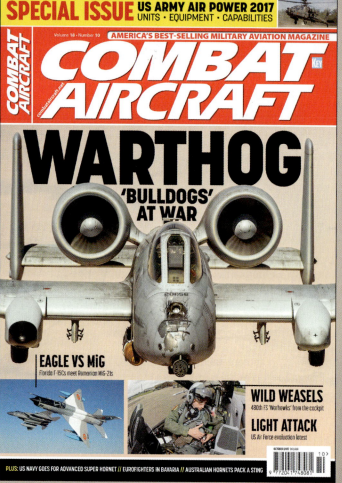

Officially The World's Number One Military Aviation Magazine...
Published monthly, AirForces Monthly is devoted entirely to modern military aircraft and their air arms. It has built up a formidable reputation worldwide by reporting from places not generally covered by other military magazines. Its world news is the best around, covering all aspects of military aviation, region by region; offering features on the strengths of the world's air forces, their conflicts, weaponry and exercises.

www.airforcesmonthly.com

America's Best-Selling Military Aviation Magazine
With in-depth editorial coverage alongside the finest imagery from the world's foremost aviation photographers, Combat Aircraft is the world's favourite military aviation magazine. With thought-provoking opinion pieces, detailed information and rare archive imagery, Combat Aircraft is your one-stop-source of military aviation news and features from across the globe.

www.combataircraft.net

The Past, Present and Future of Flight
As Britain's longest established monthly aviation journal, **Aviation News** is renowned for providing the best coverage of every branch of aviation. Each issue has the latest news and in-depth features, plus firsthand accounts from pilots putting you in the cockpit and illustrated with the very best photography. Now incorporating JETS magazine, **Aviation News** brings you the best of both magazines.

www.aviation-news.co.uk

Britain's Top-Selling Aviation Monthly
FlyPast is internationally regarded as the magazine for aviation history and heritage. Having pioneered coverage of this fascinating world of 'living history' since 1980, **FlyPast** still leads the field today. Each issue is packed with news and features on warbird preservation and restoration, museums, and the airshow scene. Subjects regularly profiled include British and American aircraft type histories.

www.flypast.com

ALSO AVAILABLE DIGITALLY:

Available on PC, Mac, Blackberry and Windows 10 from **pocketmags.com**

845/17

FOR THE LATEST SUBSCRIPTION DEALS

VISIT: www.keypublishing.com/shop

PHONE: (UK) 01780 480404 (Overseas) +44 1780 480404

On the Ark

The Admiralty's Phantoms

With both Speys in full burner 767 NAS Phantom FG.1 XT863 powers its way into the sky at RAF Abingdon on September 18, 1972. *Adrian M Balch*

From the outset, British Phantoms were designed to meet a mostly naval orientated specification. The Fleet Air Arm operated the type for just over ten years, during which time they frequently deployed aboard HMS *Ark Royal*.

In response to interest from the British Ministry of Defence (MoD) McDonnell Douglas re-designed its highly successful F-4 Phantom II to meet British requirements. These changes were mostly required by the Fleet Air Arm (FAA), which needed a new generation of jet fighter and attack aircraft to fly from carriers such as HMS *Ark Royal* and HMS *Eagle*.

The new aircraft would need to replace the de Havilland Sea Vixen in the interceptor role and the Supermarine Scimitar on ground attack missions. Furthermore, it would need to fly from the deck of ships much smaller than their US counterparts.

The cancellation of the Hawker Siddeley P.1154 [Ed: see p12] paved the way for the Navy to lay down its specifications for what was initially dubbed the F-4B(RN).

However, the Royal Navy had long been in discussions with McDonnell Douglas and an F-4B had even visited RNAS Yeovilton, Somerset in 1961 on the way home from the Paris Air Salon. The manufacturer had also noted the Navy's preference for the Rolls-Royce Spey turbofan and had begun design work to prove the engine could successfully be used within the fighter.

Additionally, it had become obvious that if the Phantom was to launch from the smaller decks of British aircraft carriers it would need to have an extendable nosewheel leg – so as to increase the angle of attack and create more lift. McDonnell Douglas had also undertaken work to prove this was feasible long before the P.1154 was actually cancelled.

The Navy placed an order for two F-4K Phantom II prototypes on July 1, 1964 and, unsurprisingly, the P.1154 project officially ended in November of the same year. The Fleet Air Arm had never been happy with the P.1154's cost, delivery schedule or its proposed BS100 engines.

Conversely, the P.1154 in its original form could have made an ideal aircraft for the RAF, but the various changes necessary to make it suitable for both Navy and Air Force use rendered it less than perfect for either air arm.

As the prototypes were being completed in Missouri the British Government announced on February 2, 1965 that the Phantom was to also equip the Royal Air Force.

Navy Prototype

The various changes to the 'standard' F-4 airframe to meet British specifications were completed in quick time – no doubt helped by the work undertaken by McDonnell Douglas before it had 'officially' received the contract.

In addition to swapping the original General Electric J79 engines for Rolls-Royce Speys and adding the extendible nose leg the FAA's F-4K had an extra fuel cell in the upper rear fuselage to counterbalance the extra weight of the AWG-10 pulse Doppler radar weapons system that was fitted in the nose. Other changes included an AJB-7 bombing system, drooped ailerons and a slotted stabilator that had reduced anhedral to enable the aircraft to rotate to a higher angle before the tail struck the deck.

The Phantom's main undercarriage was also changed and now featured 30in x 11.5in tyres (and large wheel wells to accommodate the undercarriage) as well as Goodyear brakes featuring a Hydro-Wire/Dunlop anti-skid system.

On June 27, 1966, McDonnell Douglas test pilot Joe Dobronski took the first prototype YF-4K (XT595) into the air from its maiden flight from St Louis, Missouri.

Flight testing showed the aircraft was blessed with good handling but the power of the Speys was seem to deteriorate quickly as the altitude increased. The afterburner was particularly slow to engage above 45,000ft and Rolls-Royce was set the task of making the Spey fit for purpose.

The first 'production' version of the

The Royal Navy was looking for a single aircraft to replace both the de Havilland Sea Vixen in the interceptor role and the Supermarine Scimitar on ground attack missions. *All KEY Collection unless stated*

The first prototype McDonnell Douglas YF-4K (XT595) aloft on its maiden flight on June 27, 1966. *Adrian M Balch Collection*

Phantom FG.1 XT857 was one of the two jets engaged in deck landing trials aboard the USS *Coral Sea* in 1968. It is seen here two years later undergoing test work with A&AEE. *Adrian M Balch Collection*

F-4K (XT597) flew for the first time on November 2 but a subsequent combination of engine and airframe 'tweaks' were undertaken and redesigning of the air intakes, jet nozzles and the Speys' internal workings added almost two years to the Phantom's projected entry into service.

Deck-Landing Trials

Between July 12 and August 1, 1968, two Royal Navy Phantoms were engaged in deck-landing trials at the Naval Air Test Station at Patuxent River, Maryland as well as aboard the USS *Coral Sea*, which was sailing off the coast of San Francisco, California.

Phantoms XT857 and XT597 were used for the exercise. The latter was the main aircraft with a production equivalent airframe and was fitted with the latest engines – complete with throttle gearing that switched from twelve to seven-stage compressor bleed when full reheat was engaged. The aircraft also boasted an automatic aileron droop system that used a microswitch to immediately return the ailerons to their normal position on touch down – the idea being to help create lift in the event of missing the arrestor wire and having to perform a 'bolter.'

The objectives of the trial were to prove the Phantom could use the British catapult launch system and to determine the minimum take-off speed. This proved to be just 129kts (149mph) at an airframe weight of 44,600lbs (20,230kg) and the aircraft showed itself capable of launching without losing more than the requisite 6ft (1.83m) in altitude.

Other test sorties investigated general handling and the Boundary Layer Control (BLC) system and during the three weeks of trials a total of 22 catapult launches were conducted.

Initial launches were flown with the stick held fully aft and while this proved suitable at higher speeds it was found wanting at lower airspeed. The sixth launch almost ended in disaster when the jet left the deck at 122kts (140mph) and despite full forward elevator being applied immediately the aircraft had already pitched up to 27 units of angle-of-attack (AoA) and the wing began to drop. Deft handling by the test pilot recovered the situation and subsequent launches were flown at higher speeds.

Recovering to the carrier after a sortie were made with full flap, aileron droop and 19 units of AoA. Compared to the Sea Vixen it was due to replace in Admiralty service the Phantom was considered more difficult to land aboard ship, specifically because of poor engine response times and a general lack of stability.

Further trials were conducted aboard the USS *John F Kennedy* in October 1968 to investigate a proposed 'stick feel' system. This consisted of a nylon strap connecting the control column to the instrument panel to give the pilot an indication of the optimum stick position for a catapult take-off. The strap had a Velcro 'weak-link' than enabled the test pilot to apply full after stick in the event of an emergency. The programme was abandoned after just four sorties when XT597 suffered an engine problem, but the system had already proved to be of benefit.

Following the success of the US testing, the first trials aboard a British carrier occurred in March 1969. HMS *Eagle* was selected for the sorties and although clearance was given for XT857 and XT865 to perform a number of approaches and 'rollers' the aircraft did not use the arrestor system. Cmdr Hefford DFC and Lt Cmdr Burn were the pilots involved in the *Eagle* project and they both reported favourably on the new type's characteristics.

Navy Deliveries

The first three Phantom FG.1s (as the F-4K was designated in FAA service) arrived at RNAS Yeovilton under the codename of Project *Translant* on March

ON THE ARK

Left: Compared to US Phantoms, the Royal Navy's F-4Ks were modified with an extendible nose leg to allow it to reach a greater angle of attack on take-off. The Phantom's main undercarriage was also changed and featured 30in x 11.5in tyres as well as Goodyear brakes featuring a Hydro-Wire/Dunlop anti-skid system. This is one of the four aircraft tested aboard the USS *Saratoga* in 1969 and wears the carrier's titling on the rear fuselage. **Right:** Sea Vixen XN650 escorts two of the first Phantoms to be delivered to the Royal Navy as they arrive in the UK on March 29, 1968. XN650 was the lead ship in the Simons' Sircus formation display team during 1968 and following her retirement was sold to the Cardiff Air Museum. The jet was scrapped in 1996 but the cockpit was saved.

▲ The first three Phantom FG.1s (XT858, XT859 and XT860) arrive in the UK on March 29, 1968.

▶ During the 1968 SBAC Airshow at Farnborough the Navy's set-piece began with a combined display by six Sea Vixens (belonging to Simon's Sircus team from 892 NAS) and five Hawker Siddeley Buccaneers from 809 NAS' Phoenix Five team. *Richard Cousens via Awyr Aviation Communication Ltd*

29, 1968 and were assigned to the newly commissioned 700P Sqn.

The aircraft (XT858, XT859 and XT860) were to form the backbone of 700P's intensive trials programme prior to the Phantom entering operational service with two squadrons; 767 NAS and 892 NAS.

As was to be expected the type suffered a number of teething troubles in the early days at Yeovilton. By now the US Navy had the benefit of nearly a decade's experience with the Phantom but the modifications requested by the FAA meant some of the systems needed to be fine-tuned.

The Spey continued to cause grief for both aircrew and ground-based engineers. The Constant Speed Drive Unit was particularly prone to overheating and the reheat nozzles were notoriously unreliable. The STR 70P radio altimeter also proved to give spurious and inconsistent readings and the original AN/ARN-86 TACAN had to be replaced with a Hoffman unit after just a few months.

Display Debut

While 700P was primarily engaged in proving the Phantom's capabilities and developing tactics it was given a short break from these duties in September 1968 when it was tasked with demonstrating the new type at the annual SBAC Airshow at Farnborough, Hampshire.

The Royal Navy set-piece at the show featured a combined display by six Sea Vixens (belonging to Simon's Sircus team from 892 NAS) and five Hawker Siddeley Buccaneers from 809 NAS' Phoenix Five team.

An attack sequence by Wessex helicopters then followed before the new Phantoms took centre stage. A four-ship of FG.1s from 700P – dubbed Pearson's Poppets after squadron boss Cmdr A M G Pearson – performed for the crowd before joining the Vixens and Buccaneers to 'beat up' the airfield at high speed.

The Navy, justifiably proud of its new fighters, also provided Phantoms XT891 and XT859 for a solo appearance and static display respectively.

Speed Record

The following May saw the Phantom back in the public eye once again – this time as part of a competition racing from London to New York (and back). The event, which took place between May 4–11 of that year, was conceived as a way of marking the 50th anniversary of Alcock and Brown's pioneering first non-stop crossing of the Atlantic and crews were challenged to set the fastest speed between the Post Office Tower in London and the Empire State Building in New York City. These city centre locations meant the crews would need to get to their airfields by road – or any other method of transport available to them.

Civilian entries included racing driver Stirling Moss and Mrs Sheila Scott in their respective private aircraft and British broadcaster Clement Freud decided to complete the route as a passenger on an Aer Lingus airliner.

Meanwhile, the Navy entered three Phantom FG.1s (XT858, XT860 and XT861) – with a fourth example (XT864) held in reserve – and were pitted against a pair of RAF Hawker Siddeley Harrier GR.1s. The Harriers had a much slower top speed but could operate from smaller areas close to the city centres – thus saving valuable 'commuting' time.

After a helicopter journey to the Vickers aerodrome at Wisley, Surrey, the Phantom crews launched for their transatlantic flight. The jets were refuelled – ironically by RAF Handley Page Victors – en route to NAS Floyd Bennett, close to New York's city centre. They then took motorcycles to the Empire State Building

Meanwhile, the RAF 'jump jets' had wowed crowds when they had launched

This four-ship of Navy Phantoms was among the star attractions at the 1968 SBAC Airshow at Farnborough. The aircraft involved were XT860, XT861, XT864 and XT867.
Richard Cousens via Awyr Aviation Communication Ltd

Following their combined routines at Farnborough in 1968 the assorted Navy jets then proceeded to 'beat up' the airfield at high speed – as demonstrated by XT867.
Richard Cousens via Awyr Aviation Communication Ltd

vertically from a coal yard near London's St Pancras railway station. After four air-to-air refuellings the lead aircraft, XV741 flown by Sqn Ldr Tom Lecky-Thompson, landed vertically on Manhattan Island 6 hours and 11 minutes later.

The Navy pilots were bitterly disappointed to have been beaten, so on the return leg on May 11 – codenamed Project *Royal Blue* – they were determined that at least one of them would be first home!

This time they chose to ignore the service limitations for continuous use of afterburner and 892 NAS Phantom XT858 – flown by Lt Cdr Brian Davies and navigator Lt Cdr Peter Goddard – beat the Harrier's time by a full hour.

The elapsed time from tower to tower was just 5 hours and 11 minutes and the transatlantic flight had taken just 4 hours and 46 minutes – a new Absolute World Record. During the trip the Phantom averaged a staggering 956kts (1,100mph or Mach 1.65) – including slowing down for refuelling.

Operational Training

Of course the Phantom was really a fighting machine and leaving aside publicity stunts such as Farnborough and the Transatlantic Air Race, the crews had vital work to do getting the jets ready for their service life.

Just a few months before the race 892 NAS had been officially reformed at RNAS Yeovilton on March 31, 1969. It would become the only FAA unit to fly the Phantom operationally from HMS *Ark Royal*.

892 NAS was initially commanded by Lt Cdr Brian Davies AFC and on the day it was commissioned he led a mixed formation of Sea Vixens and Phantoms to mark the 'changing of the guard.' The Phantom was considered by many at the time to be the Navy's final fixed wing aircraft; the 892 NAS therefore adopted the last letter of the Greek alphabet, Omega, as its insignia. This was worn with pride on the tail of its new aircraft but the prediction turned out to be inaccurate – in 1980 the Sea Harrier joined the FAA

and is (to date) the last fixed wing type to operate from its carriers.

The crews on the new squadron were mostly formed from a nucleus of 700P men, and many of the unit's aircraft were also drawn from the trials fleet. Air and ground staff had also received training in the USA prior to arriving at Yeovilton.

The squadron's primary task was fleet air defence and considerable training was undertaken to perfect its standard operating procedures and tactics. Crews practised intercepts at all altitudes as well as air combat manoeuvring and in-flight refuelling – the latter with RAF Victors.

In June, training began in the secondary ground attack role with Phantoms expected to be used in for close-air support during any amphibious landings. In this application the Navy Phantoms would use the same weaponry fitted to their RAF cousins; namely SNEB rocket launchers, retarded bombs and BL755 cluster bombs. However, unlike the RAF aircraft, the FG.1s were not equipped to carry the SUU-23/A gun pod.

Phantom FG.1 XT872 rolls to a halt at Wisley on May 11, 1969 at the end of its dash across the ocean during the Transatlantic Race. Despite the fact that the braking 'chute can still be seen billowing the navigator is already exiting the cockpit ready to be picked up by Wessex XS514 for the short trip to the Post Office Tower in London.

As part of its refit the *Ark Royal* was fitted with two new BS4 steam catapults that allowed launches in almost nil wind over deck conditions. To stop the aircraft at the end of their missions a series of US-built Van Zelm bridle type arrestors were fitted to each catapult. This Phantom FG.1 (XV587) was later passed to the RAF and was ultimately scrapped in 1993.

ON THE ARK

▲ The impressive Carrier Air Group embarked on the *Ark Royal* included 12 Phantoms and up to 14 Buccaneers, such as this example seen returning to the ship in 1974.

▶ An 892 NAS Phantom shares the *Ark Royal* deck with a 849B Sqn Fairey Gannet.

Left: F-4K Phantom XT872 is launched from the USS *Independence* (CV-62) during the NATO Exercise *Ocean Safari* in November 1975. *US Navy* **Right:** XT869 demonstrates the type's drooping ailerons to good effect during a slow pass at the 1969 Biggin Hill Air Fair. This aircraft was lost on October 15, 1973 when it suffered a complete hydraulic failure while landing at RAF Leuchars. *Richard Cousens via Awyr Aviation Communication Ltd*

Later in 1969 the 892 NAS crews began to practise mirror deck landings by conducting 'touch and go' rollers aboard HMS *Eagle*. All went well, but the ship's refurbishment was yet to get underway and work to get HMS *Ark Royal* ready to accept Phantoms was not due to be complete until the following March.

Therefore in October, in order to gain valuable experience at catapult launches and arrested landings at sea, 892 NAS was deployed to the USS *Saratoga*, which was cruising in the Mediterranean.

The *Saratoga* was assigned to the US Sixth Fleet and was home to VF-103's squadron of F-4J Phantoms so it was an ideal training platform for the 'green' Fleet Air Arm crews. Those selected for the deployment were swiftly sent to RAE Bedford to practise catapult launches on the runway-based 'cat' and four 892 NAS Phantoms flew out to meet the ship off the coast of Malta on October 12.

The first aircraft to land was XV567, flown by Lt Cdr Davies (the squadron CO) but the other three were delayed by poor weather. The remaining aircraft (XV568, XV569 and XV570) finally arrived on October 17, by which time they had gained USS *Saratoga* stencilling on the rear fuselage alongside their British markings.

Unexpectedly Operational

Training progressed well but soon the *Saratoga* was directed by the Commander of the Sixth Fleet to set course for the Eastern Mediterranean, where it was to conduct 'contingency operations' in response to a coup in Libya and unrest in Lebanon.

Nonetheless, FAA training continued and British crews flew alongside VF-103 Phantoms engaged in 'tactical missions' in what was formally referred to as a 'bilateral training exercise.'

Six days later a temporary stop was put to British operations after it was discovered that the blast and heat from the Phantom's Spey engines was damaging the *Saratoga's* deck! A compromise was later reached which saw the FAA jets being allowed to operate again, but only at a reduced take-off weight – something which seriously shortened each mission. Nonetheless, by the end of the deployment British Phantoms had conducted 61 launches and all the crews were declared carrier qualified.

Upon their return to Yeovilton the Phantom crews began to work with the Fairey Gannet AEW.3s of 849B Sqn, which were destined to be based alongside them on HMS *Ark Royal*. Further training followed in February 1970 when the aircraft teamed up with French Aéronavale Vought F-8 Crusaders for air combat manoeuvring off the Cornish coast.

The same month saw the *Ark* eventually emerge from its lengthy £32.5 million refit at Devonport dockyard. Work had been undertaken to extend her useful life and also make her suitable for Phantom operations. She now had an angled deck that was also extended fore and aft to accommodate the big McDonnel Douglas jets. The decision to choose an angled deck had been made specifically to suit the Phantom, which had a higher landing speed than the jets the Navy had been operating to date. Without such a modification the ship would have needed a crash barrier and arrestor nets to stop overshooting Phantoms colliding with infrastructure or other aircraft on deck.

The carrier had also been fitted with two new BS4 steam catapults – one of which was mounted on the new 199ft (60.60m) waist deck. These allowed launches in almost nil wind over deck (WOD) conditions. To stop the aircraft at the end of their missions a series of US-built Van Zelm bridle type arrestors were fitted to each catapult.

The ship's deck itself was strengthened to accept not just the weight of the big Phantoms but also to help resist the temperatures created by their reheated

Both FAA and RAF crews alike benefited from 'cross-decking' with US Navy and US Marine Corps carriers including the USS *Enterprise* and USS *Independence*. *US Navy*

XV588 launches from the Ark Royal in September 1972. The jet was written off five years later in May 18, 1977 when it caught fire during take-off from RAF Leuchars. *US Navy*

An 892 NAS Phantom landing on the USS Nimitz in 1975 during a 'cross-decking' exercise. *US Navy*

Seen aboard the USS Independence in 1974 this FAA F-4K Phantom demonstrates the relative length of its nose leg compared to a US Navy F-4J from VF-101. *US Navy*

Spey engines. If allowed to run in full reheat it was estimated that the engines could melt the deck in just 15 seconds! Water-cooled blast shields and deflector plates were also fitted behind the catapults to dissipate the heat during take-off.

Below deck the carrier could now accommodate eight Buccaneers on the lower level and eight Phantoms in the upper hangar. The latter would also house six Westland Sea Kings and three Gannets while an extension also provided accommodation for a pair of Westland Wessex helicopters.

The remaining aircraft – including up to four Phantoms and six Buccaneers – would be accommodated up on deck.

Defence Review

Navy officials had high hopes that Ted Heath's incoming Conservative Government would reverse some of the outgoing incumbent's decisions to scale back the military. Pundits predicted a reversal on the decisions to withdraw all forces from the Far East and to phase out the Navy's aircraft carriers. However, the October 1970 defence review only stated that HMS *Eagle* would serve until 1972 and the recently refitted HMS *Ark Royal* would serve until the late 1970s, but would not be replaced.

The original plan had also called for HMS *Eagle* to be modified in a similar fashion, and in many ways she would have made a better home for the F-4Ks. She had a fully angled deck, more hull life and had just emerged from a refit – but the decision was taken to only make her capable of operating Phantoms on a short-term basis and only in an emergency.

As a result the planned second squadron of Navy Phantoms was never commissioned and a number of F-4K jets on order were diverted directly to the RAF. As it happened, 892 NAS would be the first and only British Phantom squadron to operate at sea and on March 23 the unit was signed off by Rear Admiral Roberts for operational readiness.

Shortly afterwards, 892 NAS was ordered to send four of its Phantoms to the Aircraft & Armaments Experimental Establishment (A&AEE) at Boscombe Down, Wiltshire in April 1970. These aircraft were employed in extensive flying trials ahead of the unit's deployment to HMS *Ark Royal* but XV566 was lost in a fatal accident on May 3. It was the squadron's first Phantom loss.

However, there was still a job to do and on June 12 operational Royal Navy Phantoms landed on HMS *Ark Royal* for the first time. This short-term embarkation off the Scottish coast enabled crews to begin their work up before going to sea for longer periods.

Embarked on the *Ark*, the 12 Phantoms of 892 NAS formed part of an impressive Carrier Air Group (CAG) that also consisted of 14 Buccaneers, four Gannet AEW.3s, seven Sea Kings, two Search and Rescue Wessex's and a Carrier On-board Delivery variant of the Gannet.

The first full deployment began on September 4, 1970 and at the end of the month the Phantoms took part in the month-long NATO Exercise *Northern Wedding*.

However, intensive *Northern Wedding* flying between October 4-10 quickly broke the catapults and arrestor gear and the CAG had to fly back to land to allow the ship to dock for urgent repairs

Deploying with the CAG

On October 19, 1970, HMS *Ark Royal* was back at sea and the CAG began to redeploy to the ship as she sailed for the Mediterranean. This would be the first of four major embarkations and the Phantoms actually stayed aboard the *Ark* until July 1973 when she went back to Devonport for another refit. Although her 1967-1970 refit was supposed to give *Ark Royal* another ten years of service life the ship spent a considerable amount of time in dock being repaired.

ON THE ARK

▲ **XT876 was lost in a fatal accident on January 10, 1972 when it suffered a double flame-out at 31,000ft and entered a spin. The crew ejected at 15,000ft but the body of pilot Cmdr Simon Idiens was never found.**

▶ **An 892 NAS Phantom taxies in after taking the 'trap' aboard HMS *Ark Royal*. The SAR Wessex crew looks on as it maintains its vigil alongside the ship.**

In October 1969 Phantoms from 892 NAS deployed to the USS *Saratoga* to gain valuable experience at catapult launches and arrested landings at sea. The jets gained USS *Saratoga* stencilling on the rear fuselage alongside their British markings. *PRMAVIA Collection*

The *Ark Royal's* deck was strengthened to help resist the temperatures created by the Phantom's Spey engines. Water-cooled blast shields and deflector plates were also fitted behind the catapults to dissipate the heat during launch. *PRMAVIA Collection*

It would be April 1974 before she was back on line and the Phantoms reembarked in May of that year – staying aboard until November 1975. During this time some of 892 NAS' Phantoms were also seconded to the USS *Nimitz* for a period.

The third embarkation was between February and October 1976, after which *Ark Royal* went back into dock for yet more repairs – this time using parts scavenged off the now-retired HMS *Eagle*. The final deployment of 892 NAS Phantoms to HMS *Ark Royal* took place between June 1977 and November 1978.

While flying from the ship the Phantoms were primarily responsible for air defence and convoy escort missions but also practised strike missions against ship-borne and land targets as well as anti-submarine warfare and air support for amphibious landings.

During their time at sea the Phantoms demonstrated remarkable flexibility, providing strike escort for various NATO combat aircraft as well as the Navy's Buccaneers.

During Combat Air Patrol (CAP) missions its state-of-the-art radar enabled multiple targets to be tracked and engaged at long-range and during attack missions it could defend itself against the most sophisticated of opposing fighters.

As its primary task was air defence, the FG.1's weapon system was optimised for the interception role. This paired the AN/ASW-25 weapons control computer with the medium-range AIM-9 Sparrow semi-active radar-homing missile – four of which could be carried semi-recessed in the fuselage underside. Four infra-red guided AIM-9B Sidewinder short-range missiles could also be carried on the wings. In the attack role the Navy Phantoms could be armed with a combination of 500lb and 1,000lb bombs, BL755 cluster bombs, unguided rockets and even the WE.177 nuclear depth bomb if the need arose.

Aircrew Training

The news that the Navy's carrier fleet was not to be replaced had an understandingly adverse effect on aircrew recruitment. FAA fixed-wing recruitment ended in 1968 and the last Navy trained crew graduated in July 1970.

Furthermore, the disbanding of 767 NAS and Yeovilton's Fighter School in August 1972 meant that all new crews arriving after that date were provided by the RAF's Post Operational Conversion Unit Phantom Training Flight (later abbreviated to just 'Phantom Training Flight'), which formed at RAF Leuchars, Fife on September 1 of that year.

Until its disbandment 767 NAS had converted more than 100 aircrew, including most of the RAF officers of 43 Sqn and all the RN, RAF and exchange crews who flew with 892 NAS.

By the end of 1974 just 17 Navy Phantom pilots remained in the service, many of whom were already on their third tour with 892 NAS. These crews were vastly qualified in carrier operations but their RAF-trained counterparts were somewhat less capable aboard a ship – they had a steep learning curve!

Both FAA and RAF crews alike benefited from 'cross-decking' with US Navy and US Marine Corps carriers including the USS *Enterprise* and USS *Independence*. This enabled pilots and navigators to acclimatise themselves with different procedures and understand how their NATO colleagues worked in a combat environment.

Likewise, exercises with other NATO air arms were an essential part of life aboard the carrier. Some would see the *Ark Royal* engaged in mock combat against US and/or French carriers whereas others might involve aircraft from different air arms working in conjunction to support amphibious operations.

Left: Phantom FG.1 XT866 was assigned to the Phantom Post Operational Conversion Unit (PPOCU) Training Flight when photographed at the 1974 Battle of Britain Airshow at RAF Leuchars, Fife. The unit was renamed Phantom Training Flight in October 1974 and XT866 was passed to the RAF and flown by 43(F) Sqn from 1979. In July 1981 the aircraft was lost after suffering instrument failure during a night-approach to RAF Leuchars; just prior to landing it flew through the slipstream of another Phantom and the left wing hit the ground at which point both crew ejected. *Airspace Images*
Right: An 892 NAS Phantom takes on fuel from a Buccaneer as his wingman waits his turn to top up. The Buccaneers made ideal 'buddy' tankers for the fleet when operating at great distances from land bases.

Unfortunately, French carriers such as the *Clemenceau* were not configured to operate Phantoms so 892 NAS was unable to join their Gallic colleagues at sea.

Moving to Leuchars

As the RAF began to take over responsibility for the Navy's fixed wing flying in the early 1970s the end of 892 NAS' association with RNAS Yeovilton began to draw to a close. On September 5, 1972 the final Navy Phantoms left the Somerset base and relocated to RAF Leuchars. Later that month the RAF took over responsibility for the maintenance and hangarage of the Navy aircraft when they were on shore leave from HMS *Ark Royal*.

Although the RAF's Phantom FGR.2s were located at various airfields around the UK the FG.1 variants it had 'inherited' from the FAA order following the cancellation of the second Navy squadron were all located at RAF Leuchars. The decision to base the remaining Navy aircraft at the Scottish base was therefore a deliberate move to consolidate the FG.1 fleet at a single airfield.

Leuchars was now home to the Phantom Training Flight as well as 43 Sqn and 892 NAS. In November 1975 the RAF's 111 Sqn joined them and converted onto the Phantom FG.1.

Phase Out

HMS *Ark Royal's* future had been in doubt for much of the early 1970s but by 1976 it was almost certain that the big flagship aircraft carrier would not see out the decade.

The Royal Navy had been granted a new fleet of carriers to accommodate its new V/STOL Sea Harriers – and these were due to enter service in the early 1980s. Combined with the fact that *Ark Royal* was becoming increasingly unreliable and her aging equipment meant repairs were ever more difficult, the writing was on the wall for the ship. Furthermore, the RAF had already been gradually taking on the air superiority, fleet defence and attack roles of previously conducted by the FAA's Buccaneers and Phantoms.

Unsurprisingly, in late 1976 it was announced that the *Ark Royal* would be retired two years later in December 1978.

The ship and her CAG were granted permission for a farewell cruise of the Mediterranean and this came to an end on November 27, 1978 when 892 NAS' Phantoms (XT859, XT863, XT864, XT865, XT870, XT872, XV567, XV586, XV589, XV590 and XV591) flew directly to RAF St Athan, Wales where they were immediately handed over to the RAF ready to be converted into air defence aircraft.

The honour of being the last man to fly from the deck of the iconic aircraft carrier fell to Flt Lt Murdo Macleod (RAF). Joined by Lt Denis McCallum (RN) – 892 NAS' Deputy Air Engineering Officer – in the observer's seat, Phantom FG.1 XT870 flew off the deck and into the history books – along with nearly a decade of Royal Navy Phantom flying.

When it entered service the Phantom had provided the Royal Navy with quantum leap in performance compared to the Sea Vixens that it replaced. It is the most capable fighter operated by the FAA to date and while it never saw action it proved to be a formidable deterrent against Soviet fleet aggression at the height of the Cold War. ❖

The Audacious-class aircraft carrier HMS *Ark Royal* was laid down in 1943 but she was not launched until 1950 and not commissioned until five years later. She was the first aircraft carrier to be equipped with angled flight deck at its commissioning and when she was decommissioned in 1979 she was the Royal Navy's last remaining conventional catapult and arrested-landing aircraft carrier. The ship is seen here being broken up at Devonport.

While the Phantom never saw action it proved to be a formidable deterrent against Soviet fleet aggression at the height of the Cold War. Bombers and maritime patrol aircraft from the USSR frequently probed and harassed HMS *Ark Royal* when she was in international waters and the Phantom crews had an enviable 'Bear Hunting' record.

Fighting the Phantom

Air-to-Air in 'Deci'

Former Phantom navigator Ian Black recalls his detachments to the ACMI ranges at Decimomannu, where he got the opportunity to dogfight the aircraft against opponents as diverse as the F-104 Starfighter and the F-15 Eagle.

Phantom FGR.2 XV439 breaks into the circuit to land at the end of a sortie. *Ian Black*

For nearly two decades the enormous air base at Decimomannu, on the tiny Italian island of Sardinia, was a regular home to the RAF Phantom force.

'Deci', which is located just north of the main town of Cagliari in the south of the island is perhaps best described as NATO's first and only 'Super Base.'

The airfield had been built for the Regia Aeronautica Italiana in 1940 and it was home to numerous Italian squadrons until 1943 it was overrun by the Allies and became a USAAF Curtiss P-40 Warhawk base. The Martin B-26 Marauders of the USAAF Twelfth Air Force 319th Bombardment Group arrived later but it was in 1957 that the airfield really found its niche.

In April of that year the Royal Canadian Air Force established an Air Weapons Training Installation (AWTI) at Decimomannu and two years later an agreement was signed between Canada, Italy and West Germany allowing other nations to use the facilities.

Busiest Airfield

The airfield was an ideal location for 'war games.' It had an elevation of just 100ft (30m) above sea level and boasted a 2,990m (9,810ft) long runway.

Over the years the base saw a growing increase in flights with various air arms choosing to visit the AWTI and use the local ranges and airspace. Consequently, between 1970 and 2000 Decimomannu had the distinction of being one of the busiest airfields in Europe.

It was also regularly home to what was probably the greatest collection of Cold War jets ever amassed in one place.

Starting with the British it was home, on a rotational base, to the Harriers, Jaguars, Buccaneers (and later Tornado GR.1s) that spent up to four weeks at a time using the ground-attack ranges at nearby Capa Frasca. Meanwhile, the air defence fleet of Phantoms (and, subsequently, Tornado F.3s) as well as the occasional Lightning and Hawk used the base on a near constant basis for air combat and air-to-air gunnery.

FIGHTING THE PHANTOM

The 'Deci' ACMI ranges were off the western coast of Sardinia and allowed the fighters the freedom to manoeuvre in open airspace. *Ian Black*

Phantom FGR.2 XV497 from 19 Sqn gets airborne at the start of a training sortie. Aircraft from UK and RAF Germany bases were frequent visitors to Decimomannu in Sardinia and Solenzara in nearby Corsica. *Ian Black*

The Royal Navy was keen to not be left out and deployed the Sea Harrier fleet to 'Deci' on a frequent basis, as did other NATO air arms including the USAFE, the RCAF and the West German Luftwaffe – all of whom were a near permanent feature alongside the resident Italians.

The Germans were perhaps the most prolific users; quick to appreciate the Italian climate and lifestyle and scores of F-4F Phantoms and F-104 Starfighters could be seen on the line every day.

Real Time War

In the late 1970s and early '80s the Cubic Corporation had the brilliant idea of tracking fighter aircraft to replicate a 'real time' war.

At the time, virtually every fighter in NATO carried the AIM-9 Sidewinder

> **If a crew made a successful 'kill', a small electronic coffin appeared on the target on the screens in the ACMI cabin**

missile so Cubic ingeniously developed a pod that fitted into the shell of the weapon and then put a probe at the front instead of a seeker-head. Using this so-called Air Combat Manoeuvring Instrumentation (ACMI) you could now downlink aircraft parameters including missile release envelopes. All of this data would be relayed in real time to a ground display – enabling the 3D world of aerial combat to be watched live in purpose built cabins.

If a crew took a shot that was deemed to be a successful 'kill', a small electronic coffin appeared on the target on the screens in the ACMI cabin. The aircraft would then be 'kill removed' from the fight by the ground control interceptor (GCI).

An ACMI range was set up off the west coast of 'Deci' that allowed the fighters the freedom to manoeuvre in open airspace (supersonic flight was essential to maintain reality). The range was also close enough to allow meaningful training missions to be carried out followed by a quick debrief.

In my opinion, the ACMI system was pure genius. Crews could now train to a new level of realism and all they needed was to replace one sidewinder station with an ACMI pod (normally painted blue).

Carrying the SUU-23 gunpod on the centerline point, FGR.2 XV411 presents a dramatic, albeit dirty, planform for the camera. *Ian Black*

Perhaps the greatest training aid was the facility to allow the crews the chance to take simulated missile shots and then analyse the data after the flight to assess each 'kill'.

Aggressors

My first visit to the ACMI range was in November 1981 when the system was in its infancy. Having flown my Phantom the 1hr 50 minutes from Germany the engineers quickly stripped off the external fuel tanks (we had left the centreline guns behind in Wildenrath) and fitted the ACMI pods.

Each pod was numbered to allow the relevant aircraft to be recognised on screen. As it was an American-created system the USAF had a large presence on the base and the training they gave was invaluable.

Alongside the visiting USAFE fighters the Americans also had a resident deployment of Northrop F-5 Tigers from the 527th Aggressor Squadron at RAF Alconbury, Cambridgeshire.

The F-5 was similar in size to the Mikoyan-Gurevich MiG-21 *Fishbed* and their pilots were experts in Soviet doctrine. Their mission was not to win the battle but to train other NATO pilots how to fight the threat.

At this period in time the MiG-21 was still in service with the Soviet Bloc air forces, as well as the swing-wing MiG-23 *Flogger B*. However, the new MiG-29 *Fulcrum* was also just coming onto the scene; an aircraft that was be a game changer for the Soviets.

First flown in 1977, it was proof the Russians were catching up with the West. Similar in many ways to a mini F-15 Eagle, the MiG-29 could perform like a twin-engined F16 – it was a real head turner.

Using ACMI, RAF air defence crews could now adopt a 'building block' programme of training and spending two weeks at 'Deci' allowed new crews to progress from basic 'one vs one' Phantom combat to multiple aircraft scenarios against dissimilar types.

The 527th Aggressor pilots were experts at playing Soviets and – unbeknown to us at the time – most had been flying in or against actual MiGs in the Tonopah ranges in Nevada. They therefore knew an uncanny amount about the Soviet fighters' turn performance and G limits as well as the tactics the Russian crews were likely to employ.

Another beauty of the ACMI system

FIGHTING THE PHANTOM

A pair of F-5E Tiger IIs from the 527th Aggressor Squadron at Decimomannu. Flying against these aircraft gave the RAF Phantom crews a better understanding of how Soviet aircraft would be handled in combat. *USAF*

Starfighters from Canada, Italy and West Germany (illustrated) were frequent opponents during ACMI training camps at Decimomannu. *KEY Collection*

The Italian climate meant it could be hot work for aircrew, so canopies were opened and sleeves rolled up at the earliest opportunity. *Ian Black*

was how it allowed the Aggressors to replicate the characteristics of the latest Soviet missiles; it was the ultimate training tool.

Previously, Phantom crews had relied on the 'chalk and talk' method of briefing and debriefing, which was an acquired skill in itself. Prior to each mission the lead crew would put together the brief and come up with the tactics they thought were best suited against their intended adversary – clearly tactics would be different against an F-104 compared to an F-15.

With each mission lasting 30 to 45 minutes (including transit times) it meant there would be around 15–20 minutes of actual combat at the most.

Before ACMI the crews flew with notepads and frantically tried to scribble down rough 'bullet points' of what happened after each engagement. This included who took what shots, how the air picture looked at the merge and whether they thought they'd made a successful kill. Some crews opted to take large 1980s-style cassette recorders to aid the debrief but ACMI changed all this.

Now there were no arguments in the debrief – each combat engagement could be fast forwarded, paused or rewound.

A Phantom overflies Decimomannu with its blue ACMI pod clearly visible on the starboard pylon. *Ian Black*

Whilst previous debriefs had taken between 30 minutes to an hour, now combat missions flown using ACMI could take half a day to debrief as every shot was analysed and cross examined.

Crews could simulate live missile firings and get a real-time appreciation of how long the missile would take to reach the target and whether they were shooting inside the weapons release envelope. ACMI was an air defender's dream.

Perfecting Tactics

Armed with all our newfound knowledge we developed and perfected our tactics accordingly to the threat we faced. With the knowledge gained from the F-5 pilots many of us felt we should prepare for the worst!

My first visit to 'Deci' gave me ten combat sorties. The first was a 'one vs one' trip against another Phantom and the second was 'two vs one.' Then we moved on to fighting the F-5s.

During the author's second visit to the ranges the aim of the mission was to protect Harrier GR.3s and allow them to get to their simulated targets and drop their simulated ordnance. *KEY Collection*

Expanding this were missions against the F-5s and F-15 Eagles together before culminating in a big 'four vs four' fight between four Phantoms and four Eagles.

My visit also included a single mission against a pair of Canadian F-104s – and even the hard wing British Phantom looked agile against the Starfighter! The Canadians' tactic of arriving at the merge and trying to get in a quick shot proved futile as their turning circle was so huge. By the time they had re-engaged they were short of fuel and we took easy shots before they returned to base on fumes.

Being British we were allocated 'Deci' callsigns named after British cars, such as 'Bentley Formation' and 'Rolls Formation', whereas the Americans would be 'Buick Formation' and 'Chevy Formation' – or somesuch reference to the US motor industry.

Air Combat Leader

By the time of my second visit to 'Deci' in July 1983 I had nearly 600 hours on the Phantom. I was therefore deemed an 'experienced' operator and an Air Combat Leader. Having worked extensively with the Harrier force at RAF Gütersloh it was

USAF Phantoms on the 'Deci' flightline. These would often fly the adversary role for visiting RAF Phantoms. *Ian Black*

a bonus that they were conducting their annual armament camp at the same time as our air combat detachment. With tactics developing continuously, the RAFG Phantom force was now looking at what would become staple missions for the future Tornado ADV fighters. Although still in its infancy, the idea of air defence fighters working with ground attack 'mud movers' was a concept that was gaining strength on the front line.

Clearly trying to capitalise on the F-4's strengths whilst working with the Harriers was not an easy task but our biggest asset was the recently introduced Skyflash missile and our excellent AWG11/12 Westinghouse radar.

At 'Deci' we were able to develop our tactics while working with the Bitburg-based F-15s of the 525th Fighter Group (The 'Bulldogs'), which acted as the bad guys of 'Red Air.' Using the large oversea ACMI ranges we took the opportunity to develop our tactics while the F-15s took on the role of simulated MiG-29 aggressors.

Our aim was to protect the Harriers and to allow them to get to their simulated targets and drop their ordnance. Using the F-4's radar we could also give them an 'air picture' to help locate the Red Air fighters – a luxury they had never had before.

Acting as a mini airborne warning

Left: Italian F-104 Starfighters were regular dogfight partners with visiting RAF fighters at Decimonammu. This pair are seen returning to the base in formation with a Tornado F.3. *Ian Black* **Right:** Northrop F-5E Tiger II 74-1543 at Decimomannu on October 24, 1985 wearing an aggressor scheme. The nose numbers were painted in a pale blue and outlined in black to represent a Soviet Bloc aircraft. This aircraft now flies with the Moroccan Air Force. *USAF/Scott R Wilson*

FIGHTING THE PHANTOM

During the author's second visit to Decimomannu the Red Air bad guys were played by Bitburg-based F-15s of the 525th Fighter Squadron, seen here over Sardinia with an RAF Hawk. *Ian Black*

Left: "So there I was…" Debriefing the old-fashioned way following a sortie at Decimomannu. *Ian Black*
Right: The Phantom's radar was very powerful but still of Vietnam-era vintage. It was also Top Secret at the time, so photographs of RAF Phantoms with the radome open are very rare. *Ian Black*

and control system (AWACS) the lead Phantom Navigator – or indeed who ever had the best air picture – would start to give a running commentary of what he thought the opposing fighters were doing. A typical call would be: "two groups, range 28 miles showing FL300 heading south." This gave the lead Harrier pilot an idea of where the threat was and the F-4s' task was now to try to mix it with the bad guys and draw the fighters away from the mud movers. If the Red Air fighters targeted the ground attack aircraft then the escorting F-4s would need to adjust their tactics in order to protect the strike package.

Whilst in its infancy, this system provided superb training for subsequent types that entered RAF service. In reality though, the Phantom crew didn't have access to the tactical information needed to run a modern warfare scenario.

The aircraft's radar was immensely powerful in that it could detect a target the size of an F-15 at a range of up to 50 miles (80km) but it was still of Vietnam-era vintage. To fire a head-on missile required the back-seater to lock the target and that meant losing all other information on any other hostile aircraft. Once locked, the radar also alerted the target that he was illuminated (assuming they were fitted with a radar warning receiver) and this normally meant two things: the opposing aircraft would start dropping chaff or using on-board jammers in an effort to deceive the radars and break your lock – and/or start a 90-degree turn and begin aggressive manoeuvring. All of this made the F-4 crew's job as hard as possible.

The back seat of the Phantom was an ergonomic slum with very poor visibility. Add in the fact that the radar was buried between your legs behind the pilot's bulkhead and you'll see why trying to keep an air picture whilst hunched over the set and pulling up to 7G was not a pleasant experience.

Of course the opportunity was also taken to fight the F-15s on a pure 'fighter vs fighter' basis and, again, this highlighted the capability and technology gap between the ageing Phantom and the then-new king of air combat. Phantom crews had to use their cunning and two-seat philosophy to try to confuse the single seat Eagles – often successfully.

Fighting the Phantom was difficult from both the back seater and front seater perspective but it was hugely rewarding trying to wring every ounce of performance out of an aircraft that was nearly 25 years old. ❖

ROYAL AIR FORCE Aircraft & Weapons

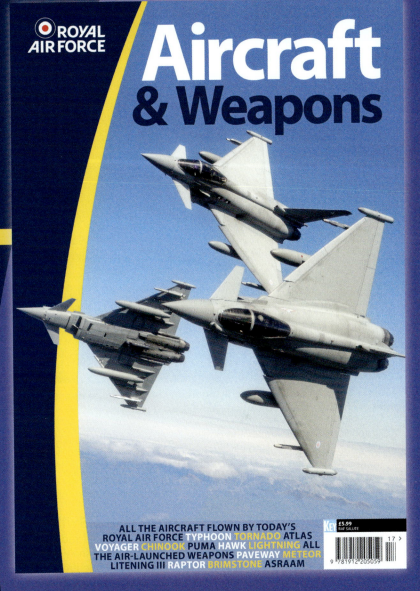

Officially endorsed by the Royal Air Force, RAF Aircraft & Weapons 2017 describes all the aircraft and weapons in current Royal Air Force service. A 100-page special magazine, it also takes a look at the RAF Regiment's vehicles and weapons, and examines some of the specialist ground equipment essential to day-to-day flying operations.

FEATURES INCLUDE:

Individual aircraft types described, with sections on role and capability, plus detailed type history

Every entry includes the very best in photography from official and industry sources

Specification, service operator and service variants tables complete every aircraft entry

Future aircraft, including P-8 Poseidon and the new UK Military Flying Training System machines are all included

Aircraft weapons, including ASRAAM, Brimstone and Storm Shadow described, with a look ahead to the long-range Meteor air-to-air missile

RAF Regiment weapons, including small arms, sniper rifles, mortars and missiles described and illustrated

Discover the RAF's awesome 30,000-litre Oshkosh off-road tanker, and container-lifting RTCH

RAF specialist ground support vehicle fleet revealed

PLUS MUCH MORE!

A **NEW** SPECIAL PUBLICATION FROM **KEY PUBLISHING**
AVAILABLE NOW FROM AND ALL LEADING NEWSAGENTS

ALTERNATIVELY, ORDER DIRECT

JUST £5.99 PLUS FREE P&P*

*Free 2nd class P&P on all UK & BFPO orders. Overseas charges apply.

Free P&P* when you order online at www.keypublishing.com/shop

OR Call UK: 01780 480404
Overseas: +44 1780 480404
Monday to Friday 9am-5:30pm GMT

SUBSCRIBERS CALL FOR YOUR £1.00 DISCOUNT! SUBSCRIBERS CALL FOR YOUR £1.00 DISCOUNT!

THE SILENT BATTLE
Phantom Electronic Warfare

Former RAF Phantom navigator **Dave Gledhill** reveals the type's now declassified Electronic Warfare capabilities.

Nothing artificial can replicate flying at low level over the sea, against an opponent intent on confusing each of your senses and corrupting your electronics. *KEY – Duncan Cubitt*

Ever popular at airshows, the British Phantom revolutionised air defence operations in the 1970s. A potent fighter, its relative lack of agility was forgiven by its two-man crew given the powerful pulse Doppler (PD) radar, eight missiles and a gun. Unacknowledged during the Cold War, its true strength lay in capabilities that were closely guarded secrets. With the Phantom fleet long since consigned to museums and the scrapman, the real story of its abilities in the invisible arena of electronic combat can now be told.

The role of the back-seater in the British Phantom was often misunderstood. With the inertial navigation system (INAS) in the F-4M or the air data computer in the F-4K at his disposal, the air defence navigator did little routine navigation, even at low level. The low flying areas became familiar and the pilot took over the burden of area navigation which typified fighter operations. Over the North Sea or in the Iceland-Faeroes Gap, a destination set into the INAS allowed quite precise station keeping during a combat air patrol and positioning was little more complex than following a range and bearing on an instrument. In the back cockpit, the role was more that of a weapons systems operator, although British navigators trained in traditional air navigation skills fiercely contested this tag.

"All Those Switches"

The AN/AWG 11 radar in the F-4K and the AN/AWG 12 in the F-4M was the key to the Phantom electronic warfare capability. Showing today's enthusiasts around the Phantom cockpit at Newark Air Museum, one of the most common questions is "what did all the switches do?" Safe to say that in respect of the little understood electronic warfare capability, many trainee Phantom navigators stared at the complex radar control panel and asked the same question.

The navigator controlled the radar in the back cockpit using three main elements. The radar display, repeated in the front cockpit, sat between his legs. The display showed the airspace ahead of the Phantom in both range and height when using the pulse mode and relative velocity when using the PD mode. An airborne intruder appeared on the basic pulse display as a fuzzy blip which was displayed relative to the host Phantom, say for example at 30 degrees left of the nose at 30 miles. Using well practised techniques ingrained during training, an intercept profile was flown to position the aircraft at a point in the sky where the pilot could use a weapon. This was achieved using verbal commands giving the pilot a heading, height and speed to fly and further controlled by commands to tighten or ease a turn or to roll and pull. The old adage, 'a peep was worth a thousand sweeps', referred to the value of a brief visual glimpse of the target against the challenge of a radar attack. On a bright blue day making an intercept was relatively easy despite the high closing velocities. On a dark, dank night with the Phantom and target flying in cloud, perhaps close to the sea, it was far more taxing.

Missile Control System

The radar hand controller allowed the navigator to set the scanner located in the nose of the Phantom in the optimum position to detect targets. Using a trigger, he could 'lock' the radar, which would then automatically track the target as it manoeuvred in space, relieving his workload. In later years, a further button

In Germany, close to the Inner German Border and threatened by Soviet Electronic Combat battalions, crews learned to be extremely frugal in using the radio during engagements. *KEY – Duncan Cubitt*

allowed him to 'interrogate' the target, looking for a friendly identification from the Identification, Friend or Foe (IFF) system. The third element of the Phantom Missile Control System (MCS) was the most important in the electronic battle. The radar control panel sat in front of the left knee and controlled the basic functions. Modes of operation, ranges and scan patterns could be set using a variety of switches but, most importantly, the panel housed the switches for the electronic protection measures, also known as electronic counter-countermeasures, or ECCM. It would be deft use of these functions that would allow the navigator to counter electronic jamming.

For the Soviet Union, the antagonist during the Cold War, electronic warfare was fundamental to its military doctrine. Electronic warfare battalions were embedded within Soviet armoured formations and the air forces were comprehensively equipped to fight in the electronic spectrum. It was expected that, if World War Three broke out, it would begin under cover of powerful electronic jamming. The invasion of Czechoslovakia in 1968 demonstrated the likely intensity as Soviet jammers obliterated the ground radars, leaving air defences forces in turmoil.

Not only were most Soviet fighters and fighter-bombers equipped with self defence jamming pods such as the *Gardeniya*, but specialist electronic combat aircraft supplemented the order of battle. The Tu-16 *Badger*, Su-24 *Fencer* and even the venerable Mil-17 *Hip* helicopter fielded specialist jamming variants which could operate in close escort or stand-off roles. Packed with complex electronic suites, the Soviet aircraft were at the leading edge of available technology and undoubtedly effective. Not only could these jammers target the Phantom's radar but they could also disrupt communications channels and jam air defence ground radars. There could be little doubt that the Phantom crews would face an intense electronic battle on 'Day One' of any conflict.

> **Deft use of ECCM allowed the navigator to counter electronic jamming**

Electronic Battlefield

The Phantom crews were expected to survive on the electronic battlefield and, to do so, in the 1970s the UK Phantoms were fitted with the Air Radio Installation (ARI) 18228 radar warning receiver designed by Marconi. Antennas mounted in the distinctive, square, fin cap gave the British Phantom a unique profile. Covering four of the major bands of the electronic spectrum, signals from ground radars, surface-to-air missile radars and air intercept radars could be detected and identified. In the rear cockpit, a display showed threat vectors from other radars which might be showing an interest in the Phantom or, more ominously, about to engage. In search mode the threat vectors pulsed, illuminating steadily when a threat locked up. Additional indicators identified different threat modes such as pulse, continuous wave and track-while-scan. An audio signal was fed into the crews' helmets, allowing the threat signal to be analysed and the attacker to be identified. Although precise identification was difficult, the unmistakable rattle of

Phantom FGR.2 XV570 stands outside its 111 Sqn HAS at RAF Leuchars on standby to launch. *KEY – Duncan Cubitt*

THE SILENT BATTLE

Phantom FGR.2 XV486 flies over a Norwegian fjord in the 1980s. *All Dave Gledhill unless stated*

Left: Phantom FGR.2 XV437 accelerates over the North Sea. **Right:** An AN/AWG12 radar extended for rectification, a procedure normally only done in a closed hangar and not on the flightline in open sight. *UK MoD Crown Copyright (1977)*

a *Fansong* radar associated with the SA-2 *Guideline* surface-to-air missile became extremely familiar, as did the more relevant air intercept radars and tail warning radars. It was these radar-equipped opponents the Phantom crews expected to encounter.

The Phantom's electronic warfare systems were principally defensive in nature. Following experiences during the Falklands conflict, defensive countermeasures systems were fitted in the 1980s in the form of the AN/ALE 40 chaff and flare system. Fitted to the inner pylons under the wing, four dispensers carried a range of infra red (IR) decoy flares and chaff cartridges which were targeted against missile seeker heads and threat radars. The navigator programmed the sequences in the back cockpit using a control panel mounted at eye level. Settings for the number of expendables, dispense timings and flare burst, namely the number of flares in a sequence, could be made. Buttons were fitted in both cockpits allowing either crewmember to dispense countermeasures at the optimum moment in air combat.

Flares were designed to confuse the IR seeker head of a hostile missile. Ejected into the airflow, providing a more attractive target, which masked the heat of the host aircraft's engines, incoming missiles were seduced into following a flight path which would pass outside the lethal radius of the incoming missile warhead. The flares were a complex cocktail of chemicals, which ignited and burned at intense temperatures giving the spectacular images captured by aviation photographers. The precise sequences to be used operationally were determined by analysts and validated during extensive testing in the air.

Chaff was designed during World War Two to confuse German air defence radars. Explosively released from the dispenser, once bloomed, the chaff bundles showed on a pulse radar as false targets. If dispensed at the correct time and coordinated with a manoeuvre, chaff can break the lock of a tracking radar and negate a missile attack. Modern chaff is a far cry from the strips of 'window' tin foil, as used during World War Two. Nowadays, tiny glass fibre strips are packed tightly in the cartridges and carefully cut to size to defeat radars operating across the frequency range.

The British Phantoms were never equipped with an active jamming pod such as the AN/ALQ 119 as fitted to the German F-4F. Principally the reason was funding as priority was given to ground attack aircraft which would operate beyond the forward edge of the battle area. There was, however, a more fundamental problem as integrating an active jammer with an air intercept radar was not a trivial task. By definition, the radar receiver which detects airborne targets is a complex and sensitive device.

◀ The distinctive square fine cap housing the radar warning receiver antennas.

▶ The effect of radar jamming on a ground radar. Sectors are blanked by the electronic noise. Discrete airborne targets outside the jammed sectors still appear.

The radar controls with the navigator's hand controller on the right. The display unit is in the centre and the radar control panel on the left.

Picking up faint electronic responses over long distances, the device is finely tuned to sense the proverbial 'needle in a haystack'. A jammer, in its crudest form emits a barrage of electronic noise which saturates a receiver making it difficult to find a target. Transmitting ten miles away from its victim, problems are presented to the air intercept radar, however, if the jammer is located under your own wing, only metres from your own radar receiver it causes havoc, flooding the receiver and making detection impossible. As a consequence, complex integration techniques are employed by manufacturers to guarantee a radar and a jammer can work in harmony.

Wobbulation

There are many types of electronic jamming, some with improbable names such as 'wobbulation'. Noise jamming was the simplest form in which the Phantom's radar emissions were amplified and returned by the jammer. This meant that the receiver was flooded and unable to process the target's return and displayed just a 'mush' of electronic noise, appearing as a spoke on the radar display. Powerful jammers could obliterate a low powered radar system rendering it unusable but the Phantom radar was better protected. Pulse Doppler radars used velocity ranging techniques and, once locked on, the target was tracked using a Velocity-Gate Pull-Off, or VGPO, techniques allowed the opposing electronic warfare officer, or EWO, to seduce the tracking gate and either break lock or send deceptive responses designed to confuse. Conversely, pulse radars used a 'range gate' providing a similar tracking function and could be seduced using range gate pull off techniques, or RGPO. Using the same basic technique, random false targets could be transmitted both in range or in velocity, baffling the navigator as to which was real and which an electronic figment.

Although the Phantom carried chaff dispensers, the crew trained to cope with the situation when the same capability was employed against them. Pulse Doppler which worked using velocity discrimination techniques was largely immune to chaff, as a chaff cloud rapidly slowed to almost zero velocity and disappeared. The older pulse radar mode was more readily seduced; carefully dispensed chaff bundles could often break a pulse radar lock. If this occurred after a Sparrow missile had been launched, because the missile relied on the continuous wave guidance signal from the main radar, it would go ballistic, missing its prey. In behind a target dispensing chaff, the crew would see a series of false targets as the chaff bundles replicated the real target. Nevertheless, a truism was that, once established in behind, the real target was always at the front of the trail. Despite the effectiveness ▶

THE SILENT BATTLE

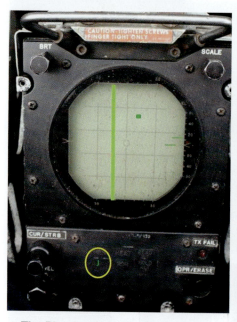

▲ The Phantom's radar display unit.

▶ The radar control panel with the electronic warfare controls highlighted.

Radar warning receiver display and controls.

The AN/ALE 40 control panel.

A Sparrow missile body with the radome removed and the seeker head visible.

Infra red decoy cartridges.

of chaff, an unfriendly EWO employing noise jamming to hide his position, learned to use chaff sparingly. Deployed at the wrong time, chaff might in fact highlight the target's position by blooming outside the protective electronic barrage instantly destroying the carefully scripted defence.

Phantom crews meeting flares dispensed from Soviet aircraft would have had varying success depending on the variant of Sidewinder carried. Soviet flares ignited in the dispenser and were burning fiercely almost as soon as they emerged into the airflow. Unlike Western dispensers which usually discharged their payloads behind and below the airframe, the Soviets fired their flares upwards. After a slow rise to peak radiance, as they fell back downwards, they would pass through the jet efflux aiming to seduce the missile seeker at that point. In the early days fielding the AIM-9G and early variants of the AIM-9L, crews were not well placed because the missile used IR guidance and both variants were easily confused by flares. Slowly, infra red counter-countermeasures were installed, initially in the form of a British modification known as SWIFT, or Sidewinder Integrated Flare Technology and later replaced with an integral electronics package upgrading the missile to AIM-9L/I standard. Both modifications improved the seeker head's resistance to flares, markedly improving the probability of a kill.

Classified Capabilities

The navigator had a range of protection measures built into the radar which he operated using the radar control panel. At the height of the Cold War taking pictures of the panel was forbidden and, even now, although examples sit openly on display in aviation museums, the real capabilities remain largely unknown. The classified supplements which described the capabilities have since been destroyed and the cine film which recorded endless training exercises passed through the shredder.

The sensitivity of the radar receiver was controlled using the 'gain' knobs with different controls for the two main modes PD and pulse. When jamming was detected, a warning light, marked 'J', illuminated on the scope alerting the navigator to the presence of electronic interference. With the gain set too high, multiple spokes would be evident across the width of the display, although the PD mode was more resistant owing to its transmitted power. By winding down the gain in pulse mode, a single spoke would remain marking the azimuth of the jammer, although the jamming still masked the range of the target. By winding the gain down still further and adjusting the angle of the radar scanner, the navigator could refine the precise azimuth and elevation of the jammer quite accurately.

The basic attack profile was known as a 'search stern', in other words a displaced stern hemisphere attack operating the radar in search mode, namely unlocked. By 'lagging' the jamming spoke around the final turn, the navigator could ensure he rolled out behind the target, although many mishandled attacks resulted in a

It would have been unusual for a Phantom to get into an up-close dogfight - but with its leading edge slats deployed its rate of turn would have made it a formidable opponent. *KEY - Duncan Cubitt*

Phantom rolling out ahead of an amused target crew. Before an intercept could be executed, the first requirement was to calculate the target's height and this was the most worrying part of the profile. In order to do so, the navigator would give commands so that the Phantom climbed to co-altitude. Those with a queasy disposition should look away. Often flown at night, to deliberately fly at the same altitude as a target coming towards you at closing speeds approaching 695kts (800mph) goes against all tenets of airmanship but that is exactly what was done. The manoeuvre was an air traffic controller's worst nightmare. Knowing the height, the Phantom climbed or descended to a height say 5,000ft (1,524m) above or below the target. At low level it was best to stay above! As the target approached, the navigator tracked the spoke manually, performing simple mental arithmetic to determine the range. When the target reached 40 degrees azimuth a gentle turn was initiated, slowly increasing the angle of bank until the navigator judged the target had passed by, at which stage the jamming strobe was brought sharply to the nose to roll out behind the jammer. Another sum determined the roll-out range but it was always reassuring to hear the pilot call a 'Tally' on the target, the codeword denoting that he had made visual contact, knowing that a visual firing could be achieved much quicker.

Counter-Countermeasures

A raft of alternative electronic counter-countermeasures were also available and described using typical military hieroglyphics, with abbreviations such as 'RSOJ','J', 'Aux J', 'Man Track 1' and 'Man Track 2'. Some of these functions were largely automatic but others required deft radar set handling from the navigator.

In order to employ the anti jamming function, jamming first had to be present. By selecting the 'J' switch on the radar control panel, highlighting the jamming strobe with the acquisition markers and squeezing the lock trigger, the radar would automatically track the jamming strobe relieving the navigator of the burden. With the radar following the jammer, basic aiming parameters were passed to the Sparrow or Skyflash missile and, along with its own protection modes, a remarkably high probability of kill could be achieved if the missile was launched under these conditions. By setting up a collision approach to

> **Flares masked the heat of the host aircraft's engines**

the target and, once more calculating the range using mental arithmetic, the navigator could position the Phantom within firing parameters in the head-on sector. In wartime conditions, one of the advantages of attacking a jamming target was that there was no doubt about its hostile intent and a missile shot could be taken freely without the need for the ground controller to declare the target hostile or the need for a visual identification by the crew.

RSOJ, or range substitution on jam, used the automatic tracking function coupled with a manually inserted target range to estimate when the target would come within the engagement envelope. Again, the Sparrow or Skyflash missile was primed with basic parameters leaving its own complex protection circuits to determine the velocity of the target. In order for the jammer to be completely effective, the attacker would have to deal with both the main radar and the missile electronics.

Auxiliary Anti-Jamming

'Aux J', or the auxiliary anti-jamming mode, was selected using another switch on the radar panel. It used the guard horn on the face of the scanner and by comparing its own signal against that of the main radar, it could identify certain advanced jamming techniques and apply corrections within the radar.

The manual tracking modes varied in complexity from the sublime to the ridiculous! Man Track 1 was relatively simple. After selecting the mode on the radar panel and squeezing the lock trigger the radar began to track a hypothetical target from the point in space nominated by the navigator. An estimated target speed was entered using the manual velocity knob and the synthetic target ran down the scope at the nominated speed. With the radar locked to the jamming strobe and an indication of potential range, the Sparrow missile was primed with estimated parameters and could be released once within the estimated engagement envelope.

Man Track 2 was truly mindboggling. Designed against more complex jammers it worked, in principle, similarly to Man Track 1 but a small vector emerged from the centre of the radar scope flicking out in a random fashion. Known as 'the wiggly worm', the navigator's job was to reinsert the vector into the centre point of the radar by moving the navigator's hand controller often in a seemingly random manner. The electronics behind the mode were lost on all but the most dedicated electronic warfare officer and the success

THE SILENT BATTLE

A 360 Sqn Canberra on approach to RAF Wildenrath. Stephan Lodewijks via Author

rates low. The mention of a Man Track 2 attack in a sortie briefing guaranteed the onset of a deep depression amongst the 'directional consultants'. It is safe to say it was little used, although far more attention may have been paid had war broken out.

One of the most effective anti jamming functions was a subsidiary display built into the main radar display and known as the 'A scope'. In PD mode this display showed a small section of the velocity spectrum around the tracking gate of the radar. In effect, the navigator could view the velocity information which he would have seen in the search mode including that of the target and use it to fight the electronic battle. When locked, the target return was still easily visible as was the velocity gate of the radar. If the two coincided, the navigator could be sure that the radar lock was solid and that his missile had a good chance of tracking to the target. If the hostile jammer employed velocity techniques such as velocity gate pull off, small 'tadpoles' would march through the real target and attempt to seduce the velocity gate onto a false target. Using the navigator's hand controller and a good deal of skill, he could coax the errant gate back onto the real target and ensure the lock held solid. A similar function was provided in pulse mode to combat range gate stealers.

Skyflash

Not only the radar employed complex protection circuits but each of the weapons had similar defences against electronic attack. The updated missile, the Skyflash, which was a British development of the Sparrow, used monopulse tracking techniques that made it inherently resistant to jamming. Both the Sparrow and Skyflash missiles were able to 'home on jam'. If jamming was detected by the missile electronics, rather than reduce the probability of kill, it acted as a beacon, attracting the Sparrow and improving the guidance and tracking.

If all had failed and despite best efforts the jammer prevented the navigator from locking on and all the Sidewinders had been used leaving just a Sparrow missile, there was one last option known as a 'boresight firing'. By selecting the boresight switch on the radar control panel and dialling in an estimated closure rate, the pilot could place the pipper on the hostile aircraft and direct a stream of continuous wave radar along which the Sparrow would guide. It was a low probability of kill under such extreme circumstances and very much a last ditch option.

The one constant was that a bullet could not be jammed and the mechanical operation of the SUU-23 was immune to electronic seduction, although if the jammer could break the Phantom's radar lock, the lead computing function built into the gunsight was rendered impotent and a fallback attack pattern was needed.

With all the elements in place, Phantom crews were exercised to employ the range of capabilities. At the most basic level, 360 Sqn Canberras, modified with ugly bulges containing numerous antennas were pressed into service as training assets. The squadron provided simple jamming training under Exercise *Profit*, also known as Exercise *Corn Cob* in RAF Germany.

The format of a sortie was relatively scripted but once jamming began, mayhem was guaranteed. In order to ensure that the radar jamming was effective, the EWO in the Canberra would 'tune' his jammer to the Phantom radar frequency. This would target the electronic noise precisely giving the Phantom crew the most effective jamming. A series of codewords identified the type of jamming against which the crew would train, the bandwidth of the requested jamming and the attack profiles. Once the Phantom navigator found the Canberra on radar, the EWO would turn on his jammer and with calls of 'sweet' and 'sour', the navigator would refine the picture to optimise the effects. Once happy, the exercise would begin.

For each intercept different techniques would be transmitted, setting different challenges for the Phantom crew. Each electronic deception required different techniques and attack profiles which were practised repeatedly. Invariably, because jamming showed hostile intent, the intercept would conclude with a missile engagement providing the navigator could overcome the electronic challenge.

It was not enough to install the complex radar warning receivers in the Phantom without providing training and this fell to the squadron electronic warfare officers or EWOs. Using synthesised sounds on an audio recorder, crews were trained to recognise the bleeps and squawks of the audio signature of, for example a High Lark radar in the *Flogger Bravo*. Engagement sequences, starting in search mode and progressing through acquisition to full track and missile launch were played repeatedly until the sounds were imprinted in the psyche. It was a brave navigator who ignored a full track lock from an SA-3 *Goa* as the result might be terminal! The downside of having the audio signal playing in the headset was that a busy and often noisy cockpit environment became even noisier. Controls in each cockpit could reduce the audio volume. Many pilots confessed to audio overload leaving a busy navigator to interpret the bleeps and squeaks.

A significant vulnerability was the radio. A VHF/UHF control box was fitted

An EW Canberra from 360 Sqn acts as a target for the author during a practice QRA scramble.

The Canberra T.17s used by 360 Sqn for electronic warfare training. Based on the B.2 they had bulges mounted on the nose to house antennas and were used to train surface-based radar and missile operators and airborne fighter and Airborne Early Warning crews in handling jamming aircraft.

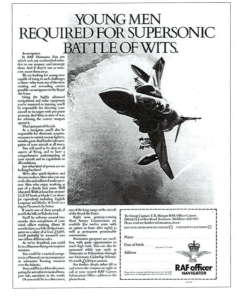

The Phantom was a capable aircraft both at day and at night.

in each cockpit, although only one box could be used at the same time. Without any electronic protection, even normal operation at high UHF frequencies were fraught. Simple jammers which scanned through the air defence frequencies and targeted the air-to-air and air-to-ground frequencies meant that normal communications were by no means guaranteed. In Germany, close to the Inner German Border and threatened by Soviet Electronic Combat battalions, crews learned to be extremely frugal in using the radio during engagements. So called 'min comms.' procedures became the norm so as not to give the opponents the chance to jam communications. Only late in the Phantom's life was the jam-resistant 'HAVEQUICK' radio fitted providing a huge improvement in capability for Gulf War operations from RAF Akrotiri in Cyprus.

Coffee Exercises

The most complex events were the coordinated jamming Exercises known as *Coffee Charlie* and *Coffee Delta*. The former pitted 360 Sqn Canberra crews against the air defence fighters whilst the latter targeted the Air Defence Ground Environment or UKADGE, the huge static air defence radars located at the Sector Operations Centres at Neatishead, Boulmer and Buchan.

Phantoms and Lightnings were scrambled to mount CAPs over the North Sea. As the Canberra crews made their ways to the start points many miles distant from the coastline, a plan had been formulated. The EWOs would target specific elements of the air defence network. The first priority might be to degrade the air picture in the Sector Operations Centre to such a degree that the battle manager might be unable to deploy his forces effectively. Another might be tasked to prevent his own Canberra from being engaged by a Phantom. A third might be to seed a

An RAF recruitment poster advertising navigator roles. *Crown Copyright UK MOD [1979]*

chaff corridor across the area further to disrupt the air picture. All would be likely to employ communications jamming that might be as simple as random noise or chatter transmitted over the tactical frequency. It may be more subtle 'spoofing' aimed to persuade unwary fighter crews to leave their combat air patrol to join a mythical tanker or to follow a false hostile target. Waves of jamming Canberras would run in towards the UK coastline. Interspersed between the jamming Canberras were 'silent' targets provided by the Canberras of No.100 Squadron serving no other purpose than to saturate the airspace. With air intercept radars often resembling Armageddon, crews experienced the type of stress probably only experienced in a Formula One car. If only the fighters were jammed, help could be provided by the fighter controller on the ground. During Exercise *Coffee Delta*, his or her own scope suffered the same barrage of electronic chaos. Whatever the effect, the coordinated effort was designed to test the robustness of the air defence forces in a silent electronic battle.

Real World Training

When accountants espouse the use of simulators to replace airborne training these exercises stand as examples of why even modern simulation can never replace the real thing. Nothing artificial can replicate the horror of flying on a dark night, at low level over the North Sea, against an opponent intent on confusing each of your senses and corrupting your electronics. The experience is 'character building' to say the least.

Whilst the descriptions of the techniques and equipment might seem technical, I have covered only the basics in simple terms. Electronic warfare uses its own language and taxes the most incisive brains. Programming jamming systems both defensively and offensively is complex and requires huge intellect and skill from personnel both in industry and at the Air Warfare Centre which provides operational support to the Front Line. Crews employing such techniques require skills and training of the highest order to be operationally effective.

At the height of The Cold War, a media campaign in the national press aimed at attracting navigators to join the RAF, showed a Phantom in a striking pose with a strap line of 'Young men required for supersonic battle of wits'. Little did those who took up the call know that, although the speeds might be a little more mundane, they would train to fight a silent war that was, indeed, the ultimate battle of wits. ❖

DAVID GLEDHILL is an aviation author of factual books about the Phantom and the Tornado F.3. He has also published a series of fictional action adventures following the exploits of a Phantom crew. If you would like to read more of his work, details of all his books can be found on his website: www.deegee-media.webnode.com

"YOU FIGHT LIKE YOU TRAIN"
Phantoms on Exercise

The old adage 'You fight like you train' has never been truer than in RAF Germany. Exercises at all levels allowed crews to hone their skills to be ready to respond to any contingency. Former Phantom navigator Dave Gledhill reveals what life was like while operating the iconic jet during a Cold War air defence exercise

Exercises held during the Cold War ranged from the exotic to the tedious, from low to high tempo and might be set in either Cold War Europe or a post-conflict South Atlantic.

'Blue' [Friendly] forces were generally those of NATO with 'Red' [Enemy] forces simulating the Warsaw Pact. Scenarios were designed to test different elements of military capability culminating in set piece events such as Exercise *Cloudy Chorus* where the entirety of the NATO structure was prepared for war.

Flying combat jets operationally was a daunting challenge and the training syllabus, whilst furnishing basic skills, did not equip crews to meet the demands of a likely wartime situation where large formations would penetrate the defences under the cover of electronic jamming. It was for planners, both at the headquarters and squadron level, to design scenarios to exercise every competence – from training in combat procedures to landing at a base to investigate its suitability as a diversion for Quick Reaction Alert (QRA) missions.

TACEVAL
One exercise drove all others as it could make or ruin careers. TACEVAL, or the annual Tactical Evaluation, was split into two parts; Part One being the readiness and generation phase, with Part Two being the full scale station evaluation, which included flying.

During the first, a 'station call out' would initiate the recall procedures ensuring sufficient personnel could be assembled to allow aircraft to be prepared, armed and placed on readiness.

Strict time limits applied in which specific percentages of the squadron's aircraft had to be made ready and declared 'on state'.

For both phases, the opening event would be a QRA scramble to ensure that the crews could meet their operational standard and be airborne within their nominated readiness time. A sure sign of the start of an exercise was the arrival of the TACEVAL evaluators at Battle Flight. The hooter would quickly follow. After a hectic few days, TACEVAL concluded with a test of procedures exploring topics such as war plans, aircraft recognition and weapons.

Other exercises led up to the 'Big One', each run by a different sponsor but aimed at the same goal.

Station Op Days targeted different training audiences from support bays to the cockpit. These 'Minivals' were run by the Station Commander and designed to train personnel from around the base in their war roles. Exercise *Maxeval* was

Phantom XV426 carrying a drill weapons load
All Via Author unless stated

A 56 Sqn Phantom crew prepare for an exercise sortie at RAF Wattisham

Invariably, evaluations were conducted in full Nuclear, Biological and Chemical protective equipment and were designed to test the system to its limits and beyond KEY – Duncan Cubitt

the next stage and was sponsored by Headquarters RAF Germany or Strike Command (later Air Command) in the UK and was the last full scale rehearsal prior to the annual evaluation. Minivals were endless and the hooter sounding at 05.00 at least once each month was a feature of life on a flying station. Hopefully, Exercise *Maxeval* occurred only once – assuming an adequate performance from everyone from the Station Commander to the Orderly Corporal.

Each exercise was administered by a team of evaluators. These might be experienced station personnel or maybe guest evaluators drawn in from other stations or headquarters. The NATO TACEVAL Team had a core staff supplemented by experts, both ground trades and aircrew, co-opted onto the team to give specialist opinion and assessment.

YOU FIGHT LIKE YOU TRAIN

Phantom XV437 flies over the snowy Norfolk countryside

Left: Phantom XV471 from 92 Sqn sitting in a hardened aircraft shelter **Right:** Groundcrew load a Sparrow missile onto the forward missile station of XV468 during operational turn-round training

Invariably, evaluations were conducted in full Nuclear, Biological and Chemical (NBC) protective equipment and were designed to test the system to its limits and beyond.

Practicing Procedures

Interspersed between the evaluations were events designed to give practice in certain procedures. Again, the scenarios ranged from relatively focused flying exercises such as Exercise *Hammer Blow* or *Mallet Blow* to major tests of the UK air defence system such as Exercise *Elder Forest* and Exercise *Priory*.

The former followed a standard script. Start points were established on the North Norfolk coast and fighter-bombers headed up the East Coast where they would be engaged by Combat Air Patrols (CAP) over the North Sea. A high-speed corridor allowed participants to fly at supersonic speeds at low level.

Off Newcastle, they would head inland routing through Northumberland at low level towards the Spadeadam Electronic Warfare Training Range that offered the means to conduct tactical training against ground threats ranged across Cumbria.

> **Hopefully, Exercise *Maxeval* occurred only once - assuming an adequate performance from everyone from the Station Commander to the Orderly Corporal**

Surface-to-air missile systems (often the real thing after the Berlin Wall fell) replicated the tactics of a potential enemy. Targets on the range offered crews highly realistic simulations against which to practise attack profiles, ranging from buildings to a simulated airfield complete with decommissioned aircraft.

Once clear of Spadeadam, the offensive formations would head southerly, through the busy air traffic control zones of the Midlands before entering the Welsh low flying area where further CAPs were positioned.

Harried by Phantoms and occasionally Hawks throughout their ingress, the culmination might be a first run attack against a ground target on one of the Welsh air-to-ground ranges, dropping practice weapons before returning to base at low level. If the sortie had been particularly aggressive, a transit through the airways at medium level might be needed in order to conserve fuel.

For the major exercises, life in the cockpit ranged from the spectacular to the dreary. If the sortie fell on the final day of the exercise – at which point the massed bomber raids were launched, the sortie might be short and hectic. With weapons expenditure being practised, it was not unknown to claim eight missile shots and a guns kill and return to base after barely an hour in the air. Equally, pulling the night shift knowing that, probably, the only other aircraft airborne was a lone 100 Sqn Canberra which would drone endlessly through the CAP area at medium level, could be soul destroying. Sometimes, a three-hour night sortie supported by air-to-air refuelling might end with a Phantom crew seeing not even a single target.

A 100 Sqn Canberra target-towing aircraft

Left: Phantom XV500 from 56 Sqn visits RAF Wildenrath during Exercise Phantom Leap

Right: Phantom XV409 lands after a TACEVAL sortie

Exercise *Guest Flint*

A major limitation was that in exercising the big scenarios at station level and higher, the key element of flying and fighting the Phantom could be forgotten. Crews might sit in vain on CAP for hours waiting for a target to intercept, meanwhile, an attack by fighter-bombers on the Phantom's own base might have bypassed the CAP area after being tasked on another conflicting mission objective.

For that reason, many squadrons turned to internally generated flying exercises focused on the task in the air. Exercise *Guest Flint*, which the author conceived, was one such exercise. The aim was to provide high quality, mixed fighter force training focusing on cockpit skills rather than the ground play typical of other events. The idea was to pit the Phantoms from the Wildenrath Wing against the SEPECAT Jaguars of the Brüggen Wing while coordinating the flying programmes so that the flying effort was focused into two major waves during the day.

This would give time for lengthy briefings and rigorous debriefings but, more importantly, would ensure the maximum numbers of combat aircraft flew through the operational areas at the same time.

By the end of the exercise, which would build up in intensity as the week progressed, the Brüggen Wing would launch large formations around a circular route, originating and finishing at Brüggen to realistic represent attacking formations. The route would head out from the so-called 'Clutch' airfields, through the Dormagen Gap between Cologne and Bonn, into Low Flying Area (LFA) 3. The undulating terrain was a challenge in terms of low flying and was sufficiently mountainous to provide terrain screening which could be used to screen the attackers from the fighters.

Heading north past Gütersloh, the attacking formations would enter LFA 1 in the Hannover area and head back westwards across the flat North German Plain towards Nordhorn bombing range on the Dutch border. After a simulated bombing run, the formations would route south-westerly through LFA 2 returning to their base. Initially four-ships would route through at 15-minute intervals. Ultimately, for the final set piece sortie, a 36-ship 'gorilla' would pass through within minutes.

Four CAP areas were established and these were manned by mixed formations of RAF or German Phantoms, USAF F-15s and American, Belgian or Dutch F-16s. Occasionally, other types such as Northrop F-5s, Lockheed F-104s, English Electric Lightnings and other F-4Fs supplemented the exercise.

Although the British Phantoms normally operated with wingmen of their own type it was not unusual, when non-pulse Doppler equipped fighters were involved, for the F-4s to split and take one of these aircraft as a wingman in order to lead them into the fight. In the early days of its deployment, it was not unknown for the Phantom to lead an F-15 into the fight, despite the latter's capable (albeit immature at that time) radar, leaving the American pilot to concentrate on the demands of flying at low level.

'Blue' on 'Red'

After a low-level transit the fighters would establish a CAP and await the arrival of the ground attack packages. The tactical lead was conferred on the aircrew with first radar contact.

With an attack plan nominated, the split formations would enter the engagement targeting individual elements of the opposing formation. Depending on the phase of the sortie the attackers would

YOU FIGHT LIKE YOU TRAIN

Wearing NBC protective clothing, groundcrew members pull a Phantom from a hardened shelter during an exercise. *KEY – Duncan Cubitt*

react in differing ways. Prior to reaching a target (and simulating a heavy bomb load) the Jaguars were less likely to respond aggressively. Post target, a robust defensive reaction was almost inevitable. The aim was for the fighters to position for a simulated missile or gun kill, and most importantly, to record the event on film. The aim for the bomber crews was to avoid a missile shot being claimed. Occasionally the tables were turned when a badly executed intercept meant a fighter rolled out in the gunsight of an appreciative bomber pilot.

The Jaguars proved to be worthy opponents and the pilots extracted every gram of performance from the venerable machine. As the exercise gained credibility, Buccaneers and Jaguars from RAF Laarbruch supplemented the ground attack force, offering increasingly varied training possibilities. A series of ancillary exercises were also tagged on. Airfield attacks by the Jaguars against Wildenrath were approved by a sometimes reluctant OC Operations Wing (despite the obvious training value, plus the positive impact on morale of station personnel seeing the Phantoms in action, the local population could be vociferous in complaining about jet noise and approval was granted sparingly). Normally protected by the Rapier surface-to-air missiles manning a base defence zone, the scenario simulated the rapiers having 'fired out' and, as a consequence, the Jaguars were met by 'Base CAPs' flown by the resident Phantoms.

In the event of bad weather preventing low flying, air combat training was conducted at medium level providing invaluable opportunities to hone vital skills. Air combat could only be flown after a face-to-face briefing so the opportunity

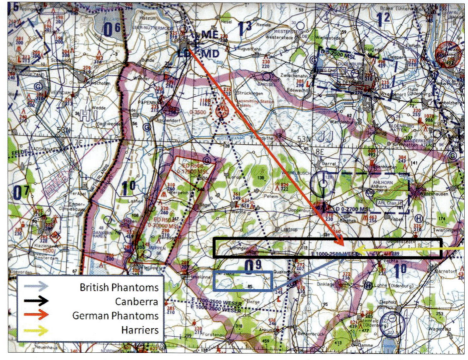

to engage in two versus two air combat against F-15s was not to be missed. This same restriction for complex exercises meant that the air defence crews had the chance to fly from the same airfield and to brief, debrief and reconstruct engagements together. At the end of the phase, a mass debrief, including the Jaguar pilots, delved into the lessons learned before the participants returned to their home bases, via the Officers' Mess bar, naturally.

Close Call

Mishaps were rare but the enthusiasm of an exercise planner on one occasion almost caused the loss of a crew and an aircraft and, given that it was my own aircraft, it became very personal.

▲ **A map showing the relative positions of the formations in the incident described in the text**

Exercise *Cold Fire* was a joint exercise held annually in the NATO Central Region. Centred around a hypothetical but realistic Warsaw Pact invasion scenario, land forces sought to stem an advance by Soviet forces into the British Army of the Rhine area along the Inner German Border. Streams of offensive support aircraft were launched, some to support the ground troops and others to attack NATO targets along the simulated forward edge of the battle area.

The Wildenrath Phantoms were tasked to mount a CAP in one of the regular operating areas over the North German

Crews prepare for a training sortie while wearing cumbersome NBC masks and suits KEY – Duncan Cubitt

Plain, particularly relevant in that wartime CAPs would have been mounted in the same area. Joining CAP with four Phantoms (a pair from each squadron), enthusiasm was high as the weather was unexpectedly fine with visibility to the moon.

It was not long before the first attacking formation flew through from east to west and a satisfying engagement ensued as crews manoeuvred for simulated kills. Re-established on CAP, the next intercept proved to be a lone Canberra which was intended to increase the workload of the fighter crews by its presence. Rather than a single run through the area, the Canberra remained in close proximity to the CAP setting up a short racetrack, returning repeatedly.

Instead of running through at low-level, the planner had deconflicted in height rather than time and the Canberra flew its profile at 1,000ft (305m) in order to be clear of any fighter-bombers operating 'on the deck' and to remain clear of the fighters' CAP height. There was little leeway given that the Phantoms were patrolling at 1,500ft (458m), the ground attack aircraft were ingressing at 250ft (76m) and everyone was sandwiched below the general aviation block which stretched from 2,000ft to 5,000ft (610m to 1,524m). The airspace was tight and it was to be a decision with near fatal consequences because the planner had set one more challenge.

As the Canberra ran westwards it was closely followed by a four-ship of Harriers which had just exited from the exercise area and rapidly overtook the slower aircraft. Simultaneously, a four-ship of German F-4F Phantoms entered the fray from the north, tasked to provide offensive counter-air against the Wildenrath Phantoms.

Ironically, that took the number of jets in the area to an unlucky 13 – and they merged simultaneously. The RAF Phantoms were intent on claiming kills on the Harriers who, divested of their bomb load, countered defensively. The German Phantoms, keen to score a kill on a busy RAF Phantom crew, entered the writhing mass of aircraft and a 'fur ball' developed at low level. It was at that exact moment when the Canberra passed through the skirmish. Threatened by a German Phantom and with the radar warning receiver blaring through the headset, I recall the canopy filling with the planform of the huge Canberra as we pulled around for a simulated shot on a Harrier. The incident was over in flash but the expletives in the cockpit went on for some moments more and the palpitations for even longer. In the heat of the fight, a mid-air collision had been averted by mere feet. The engagement was terminated using the universal sign of 'waggling the wings' and a return to the CAP datum initiated. A tense discussion on the tactical frequency followed as the German Phantoms snapped at our heels, probably calling our heritage into question given our reluctance to fight.

The intent was laudable. The planner coordinated the exercise activity to offer highly realistic training value. Apart from the Canberra's presence, thereby saturating the airspace, the scenario was sound. One extra aircraft tipped the scales to the point of danger. With the risk of collision high we opted for a premature return to base in order to live to fight another day. Usually our recovery would be on fuel minimums. That day there was a surfeit of spare Avtur. The transit back through the low flying area was subdued, in stark contrast to the usual adrenaline stoked 'high' which would follow a demanding engagement. Happily such incidents were rare.

The old adage says that 'You fight like you train'. Exercises at all levels allowed crews to hone their skills to be ready to respond to any contingency. Thankfully, the skills needed to fight World War Three were never put to the ultimate test. Hard won expertise was never examined for real and the Cold War ended peacefully.

> **Thankfully, the skills needed to fight World War Three were never put to the ultimate test**

Nowadays, with tensions purportedly eased, the call-out hooters are silent and full-scale exercises in chemical conditions are a distant memory. Nevertheless, real world events have ensured that operational aircrew will always be honed by exercising their skills and capabilities and stand ready if called.

DAVID GLEDHILL is an aviation author of factual books about the Phantom and the Tornado F.3. He has also published a series of fictional action adventures following the exploits of a Phantom crew. If you would like to read more of his work, details of all his books can be found on his website: www.deegee-media.webnode.com

Black Mike
A Very Special Survivor

Phantom XV582 was the first of the British Phantoms to exceed 5,000 flying hours but it also set a world speed record and is famed for wearing one of the most dramatic special schemes to ever adorn a Phantom. Today, Black Mike is a rare survivor with an exciting future.

With Flt Lt Gordon Moulds at the controls, XV582 overflies the Forth Bridges during her 1990 display season. *All KEY – Duncan Cubitt unless stated*

On February 24, 1988 43 (F) Sqn Phantom FG.1 XV582/'AF' appeared overhead Lands' End in Cornwall at a high rate of knots. At the helm was Wing Cmdr J Brady (the squadron's 'boss') and navigator Sqn Ldr M Pugh-Davies and just 46 minutes and 44 seconds earlier they had been 603 miles away, over John O'Groats in Scotland. The flight easily achieved a new FAI world speed record that averaged more than 658kts (757mph) and remains unbroken almost 30 years later.

Coincidentally, during that high-speed run over the length of the United Kingdom XV582 also became the first British Phantom to exceed 5,000 flying hours. The RAF Leuchars, Fife-based aircraft had already earned its place in history – but more was still to come.

In due course, XV582 moved across the airfield and was passed from 43 Sqn into the care of 111 Sqn. In service with 'Treble One' the jet was re-coded 'M for Mike' and initially retained its standard Air Defence grey scheme.

However, in the late 1980s members of the squadron began giving thought to painting one of its jets in a special commemorative scheme to mark the unit's 70th anniversary in 1987.

In the 1950s 'Treble One' had famously operated the Black Arrows teams of gloss black-painted Hawker Hunters at airshows and a plan was hatched to apply this distinctive scheme to a Phantom. As it happens, the plan never came to fruition but two years later, in late spring 1989, Wing Cmdr Terry Hanlon decided to revive the project to mark both the final year of RAF Phantom FG.1 service and the 30th anniversary of the Black Arrows.

The scheme would comprise of an all-over gloss black airframe with 111 Sqn's crossed swords emblem on the tail and a golden lightning bolt on the front fuselage. Furthermore, it was decided the jet that would gain this scheme would be the record breaking XV582.

Ground crew from RAF Leuchars spent many hours rubbing down the previous layers of green and grey camouflage on XV582 to get a smooth surface for the undercoat. They then applied a high gloss black topcoat before applying the special markings and adding XV582's individual code letter 'M' to the fin in bright red.

Unsurprisingly, XV582 was soon dubbed 'Black Mike' and the jet made its debut at the press preview ahead of the RAF Leuchars Battle of Britain Airshow on September 23, 1989.

Display Jet

Originally, Black Mike was to be a static star at the airshow and would revert to its standard grey scheme soon after the event. However, public interest in the distinctive jet led to a rethink.

A request to fly the Phantom in this non-standard scheme was passed up the chain of command until it reached Commander-in-Chief of RAF Strike Command, Air Marshal Sir Patrick Hine. As it happened, Hine was an ex-Black Arrow. Furthermore, he wanted to fly Black Mike himself and the appeal to retain XV582's stylish black scheme was soon approved.

The RAF saw the public relations benefit of demonstrating Black Mike to a wider audience but XV582 was nearing the end of its fatigue life and only had around 50 hours left on the airframe. Nonetheless, it was decided to use up those hours by visiting various airshows during the 1990 season.

BLACK MIKE

Black Mike takes on fuel from Victor K.2 XL512. The Victor was scrapped in 1993 but the Phantom is one of aviation's lucky survivors.

Through the 1990 airshow season Black Mike was seen at various aviation events around the UK. It was then retired to Leuchars and was a regular participant in the static park at the base's annual airshow.

Flt Lt Gordon Moulds, an instructor with 228 OCU at Leuchars, was chosen to fly Black Mike and she appeared at more than a dozen displays across the UK before finally being retired and placed on gate guardian duties at Treble One's base.

Preserved

Following her retirement, Black Mike remained outside 111 Sqn's offices at Leuchars until the squadron disbanded in March 2011. It was then moved into storage in a Hardened Aircraft Shelter (HAS) at Leuchars but was wheeled out once a year to appear on static at the station's annual airshow.

In 2013 it was announced that Leuchars would close as an air base and transfer into the hands of the Army.

It was at this point that XV582 was put up for disposal and came to the attention of the British Phantom Aviation Group (BPAG). Initial fundraising went well until sadly one member disappeared with almost £11,000 of donated funds! Distraught but undeterred the volunteers began to look at other options to save this unique aircraft.

Fortunately, Gary Spoors of GJD Services stepped up to the mark and purchased the Phantom on behalf of the group, which will repay his costs as quickly as possible.

This generosity has enabled the BPAG volunteers to begin work disassembling the jet ready to move it south from Leuchars.

Despite numerous approaches and

Black Mike comes over the coast just prior to landing at RAF Leuchars in the spring of 1990.

negotiations with the highway authorities, it has proved impossible to transport the aircraft with the wing and fuselage still as one unit – but how do you take a Phantom apart, when you absolutely don't want to cut it?

Well, you ask around, plus BPAG are lucky to have the support and knowledge of Ulster Aviation Society, who recently moved another Phantom from Leuchars. Furthermore, a BPAG member also had first hand experience of dismantling Phantoms.

BPAG's Paul Wright picks up the story: "Our volunteers applied themselves to the head scratching, knuckle bashing and drill re-sharpening task of removing a plethora of panels. They also removed the tail assembly and a seemingly endless array of minor brackets and sub systems that crossed the wing/fuselage boundary. Almost 30 years of sitting near the North Sea have had an effect on the stressed skin aircraft and meant that almost every single fastener fought against our efforts to remove it. In the end, many hundreds of fasteners simply had to be drilled off.

"Despite good progress, another headache loomed steadily up, one which just wouldn't go away – the engines would have to come out!

"Access to the structure and main mounting bolts in the engine bays just wasn't possible with the powerplants fitted – however, despite much searching by ourselves and Everett Aero, no engine removal gear could be found.

"It was at this point that we reverted to some good old British ingenuity in the face of adversity. A set of removal gear was fabricated in the engineering shop of a theme park in South Wales, to fit a Conway engine stand situated in Leicestershire, to remove two Spey engines situated in Scotland... and it worked! It took a bit of grunting and a little nervous sweating, but it worked. For the first time in around 25 years the

Left: XV582 was painted gloss black paint in homage to the famous 111 Sqn Black Arrows Hunter team. It also gained 'Treble One's' crossed swords emblem on the tail and a golden lightning bolt on the front fuselage. **Right:** Gordon Moulds plugs in the burners and brightens up the dusk skies over the Scottish highlands.

engines were out and a major milestone had been passed."

Dismantling any aeroplane can be a trying experience, and one situated on an active MoD base comes with its own challenges. BPAG visits had to be coincided with Leuchars' exercises and day-to-day military activity but the group has built up a good rapport with the Station Staff Officer, whose assistance with accommodation, passes and access, made the task less difficult.

Volunteer Force

The work undertaken on Black Mike to date has been done by a group of dedicated volunteers. Some worked on Phantoms in the RAF and wanted to relive their youth, others worked on other types in the RAF and many were 'just' civilians who just wanted to say they'd worked on a Phantom. "It didn't matter what their reason was," explains Paul, "they all pitched up, all at their own expense, taking holiday time, braving the cold of Leuchars (there's no heating in the HAS, which is just feet from the North Sea!), and the usual 'nips' and 'bites' that a Phantom will give you. We thank them all; without your dedication, none of this would've been possible. It would also be remiss to not pass on our greatest thanks to the guys at AHF/VASS (Aircraft Servicing Flight/Visiting Aircraft Servicing Section) RAF Leuchars, for all their help and tea."

At the time of writing [in late September 2017] the Phantom's outer wings are off for road transportation, all the attaching structural components and trailing edge flaps are removed and all the major bolts are either loose or out. The next step is to carefully lift the whole aircraft up and support the fuselage as the wing is lowered from underneath it. Once that's done, it's over to GJD Services to arrange road haulage to XV582's new resting place, along with dozens of boxes of removed components and structure.

New Home

The original plan had called for Black Mike to move to Bruntingthorpe, Leicestershire for restoration and preservation but earlier this year Gary Spoors was approached by the RAF to ask if the Phantom would be available to be displayed at RAF Cosford as part of the centenary celebrations in April 2018.

As such, the jet will soon be transported from Fife to the museum in Shropshire, where it will reside for the winter whilst being renovated for public display.

After that, it will be moved to its new home, and the real work starts. "We're planning a full paint strip followed by a wingtip to wingtip, nose to tail inspection inside and out," says Paul. "We'll also be rebuilding and replacing everything that was stripped out for the road move as well as testing the systems. This is far from a short-term project but we do intend to start public access as soon as practical though, starting with guided tours of the restoration work."

Just a handful of British Phantoms have survived the scrapman [Ed: see p96]. The acquiring, dismantling, moving and preserving of an aircraft as large and complex as a McDonnell Douglas F-4 Phantom is a major undertaking for any organisation – let alone a small group of volunteers that has limited access to specialist tooling and relies on unpaid manpower. The work undertaken to date has required some very lateral thinking at times and the BPAG is to be praised for sticking with the project during good times and bad. Through their hard work Phantom XV582 is set to delight a whole new generation of enthusiasts.

If you'd like to get involved in any way, please e-mail Paul on britishphantomaviationgroup@gmail.com. ❖

> The Editor would like to thank BPAG's Paul Wright and David Butterfield for their assistance while preparing this feature.

Work to dismantle Black Mike at Leuchars has been undertaken by a team of enthusiastic volunteers. Some have an RAF background whereas others are civilians who welcome the chance to work on a Phantom. *Via BPAG*

Once the wings are removed XV582 is due to be roaded to RAF Cosford, Shropshire for ongoing restoration and temporary display as part of the RAF Centenary celebrations. *Via BPAG*

BIG CAT HUNTING

The British Phantom's Only Air-to-Air Kill

The RAF Phantom fleet only scored one air-to-air victory – but it was not a celebrated event, as **Ian Black** reveals

May 25, 1982 is a memorable day in RAF history for all the wrong reasons. News was filtering back to the UK that the *Atlantic Conveyor* transport ship had been hit by Exocet missiles en route to the Falkland Islands. It was a terrible blow to the campaign with its huge stocks of ammunition and vital Chinook and Wessex helicopters on board.

Perhaps this tragedy masked what was a further hammer blow to the RAF's history, which occurred thousands of miles away on the same day.

Back in Europe the RAF was on constant alert for a war that thankfully never happened. The Cold War was reaching its peak – the tension between West and East was at its highest in the central plains of West Germany and the area between Bonn and Berlin was the virtual battleground between two of the largest armed forces ever seen on the brink of all out nuclear war on a daily basis. The training was equally intense and the thought of conflict very real. It wasn't a question of 'if' the war would happen it was more a case of 'when.'

Toned Down

Amid this tension McDonnell Douglas Phantom FGR.2 XV422 was to become one of the RAF's most famous Phantoms – for all the wrong reason. The aircraft was a single-stick Phantom and by now was on strength with 92 Sqn at RAF Wildenrath as an air defence fighter. XV422 had previously served much of its career in the ground attack role with 31 Sqn 'up the road' at RAF Brüggen. It then briefly flew with 23 Sqn in the UK before returning to RAF Germany to join 92 Sqn as aircraft 'O'.

The jet's initial claim to fame was purely cosmetic, as it became one of the first RAF 'Barley Grey' air defence Phantoms. It was part of a trial scheme that saw a handful of the RAFs F-4s painted in a low visibility camouflage with toned down national markings and insignia.

It was now some years since its repaint though and it was clear the matt finish was not wearing well – XV422 was one of the most 'worn' looking airframes in service.

War Footing

The relative calm of Cold War life had taken a dramatic new twist in the previous month. Having trained for a conflict against the Warsaw Pact, the RAF was now deploying to a theatre far removed from Eastern Europe. After years of peacetime operations the RAF was on a war footing, albeit in the South Atlantic.

As the sun rose on May 25, 1982 the

That morning 92 Sqn already had three airframes fully armed for Battle Flight duties at Wildenrath – two aircraft 'on state' and ready to launch from the HAS with five minute's notice plus a spare.
All via Ian Black

XV422 served much of its career in the ground attack role with 31 Sqn but briefly flew with 23 Sqn where it was coded 'C'.

Awaiting the call to stand down... or scramble.

RAF Wildenrath silence was broken by the banshee wail of the alert sirens calling air and ground crews to work for one of the many 'generation' exercises. These were in-house exercises to prepare the units for TACEVAL (Tactical evaluation) by NATO – and they were taken very seriously.

The pattern was the same – crews would rush to the squadron collecting their NBC (Nuclear Biological Chemical) warfare suits and report for duty. The aircrew immediately entered the special hardened Pilots Briefing Facility (PBF) and began preparing for simulated 'live' missions. Weapons would be drawn, flying clothing prepared and war plan briefings commenced for both 'SUPPLAN Mike' and 'SUPPLAN Delta.' These were complex rules that air defence crews used to engage hostile targets whilst integrating with the low and high level surface-to-air (SAM) systems. They were very complex procedures that required crews to be totally disciplined.

Generating Aircraft

Meanwhile, the ground crews began the thankless task of 'generating' aircraft – i.e. repairing unserviceable aircraft and arming as many Phantoms with a full war fit in as short a time as possible.

That morning 92 Sqn already had three airframes fully armed for Battle Flight duties at Wildenrath – two aircraft 'on state' and ready to launch with five minute's notice plus a spare. Nevertheless, the task for the engineers was tough. Missiles were normally stored at secure locations and they would need to be delivered to their respective Hardened Aircraft Shelter (HAS) where armourers would load the weapons onto serviceable airframes.

Once loaded, various safety checks would take place to confirm that the missiles were correctly loaded and there

" It was highly unusual to be scrambled with live weapons "

were no stray electrics that could cause an accidental firing. At this stage crews would leave the hardened PBF area and walk to their assigned aircraft in the various shelters around the dispersal.

On arrival, after a thorough check of the airframe and its missiles, they would sign for their aircraft, making careful note of the live weapons fitted. The pilot and

BIG CAT HUNTING

XV422 had been part of a trial scheme that saw a handful of the RAFs F-4s painted in a low visibility camouflage with toned down national markings and insignia. By 1982 it had been some years since its repaint and it was one of the most 'worn' looking airframes in service.

RAF Germany was equipped with a mixture of aeroplanes. The Jaguar was very much at home at low level over the German countryside, but from certain angles it was very easy to confuse it with the MiG-23/27 family.

The Phantom could carry an impressive array of missiles but at the end of the TACEVAL the armourers normally unloaded all the missiles and returning the aircraft to a 'training fit'.

navigator then strapped in and called "cockpit ready." At this stage the aircraft was fully armed, fuelled, serviceable and ready to scramble – it was therefore considered 'on state.'

Once 70% of the unit was on state the exercise would normally be terminated and normal life was resumed. For the armourers this now meant unloading all the missiles and returning the aircraft to a 'training fit' (normally centre line gun with no bullets, a training Sidewinder with a seeker head to acquire targets but no rocket motor or warhead and a small 'plug' that simulated the carriage of an AIM-7 Sparrow).

Live Aircraft

However, on May 25, 1982, for reasons that are unclear, the Commanding Officer at Wildenrath decided not to disarm the Phantoms but scramble them off to perform training missions in the low flying areas.

During this era the RAF Phantom ruled the skies in Germany – it boasted a fearsome weapon load and a very capable pulse Doppler radar. In those carefree yet tense days standard operating procedures allowed NATO fighters to roam freely around the low flying area of Germany intercepting Targets of Opportunity from any NATO air arm.

" There was a loud explosion and the Jaguar rapidly lost control "

Loose rules allowed the aircraft and their 'targets' to engage each other at low level in mock combat – with two 360° turns and one reversal turn permitted. Nevertheless, in the thick of mock combat the actual figures got lost and full blooded air battles took place – training was never more realistic!

These were un-briefed dogfights with no communications apart from the unwritten rule that either side could waggle their wings meaning the engagement was terminated.

Under normal circumstances air defence crews only flew armed aircraft on Battle Flight scrambles, missile camps or gunnery camps but on this day safety procedures were also in place to prevent accidental firing. In the cockpit the armourers were supposed to apply a cross of white tape over the Master Arm switch to prevent the pilot from finally arming the aircraft. Furthermore, in the rear cockpit the navigator was responsible for pulling a Circuit Breaker (CB) using a special tool to render the armament circuit inoperative. Finally, the GCI (Ground control Interception) would be alerted that they were working with live armed aircraft and prior to each intercept the controller would ask: "confirm switches safe?"

Scramble!

Sat in their concrete HAS the crew of XV422 awaited further instructions. Having been told the exercise was terminated they expected a quick walk back to the squadron so they were probably startled when their radios crackled into life and Sector Operations called "Mike Lima 67 Scramble Scramble Scramble vector 030 contact Crabtree on TAD 468."

It was highly unusual to be scrambled with live weapons but the crew were both experienced air defence operators and thought little of it. In accordance with procedures the navigator pulled the relevant CB and assumed the Phantom was now unable to fire weapons in anger.

Quickly airborne the Phantom started a hard turn through 180° to avoid Dutch Airspace (Wildenrath was literally a few kilometres from the German Dutch Border) and then the crew quickly ran through what they had done hundreds of times before. ➥

BIG CAT HUNTING

On May 25, 1982 SEPECAT Jaguar GR.1 XX963/AL was returning to its base when the unthinkable happened. It is seen here landing just two months earlier.

The back seater's office in an RAF Phantom.

The wreckage of XX963 came to rest in open farmland 50 miles from its base.

The backseater pulled out his radar and started looking for 'trade' (the term for unknown targets) whilst the pilot focused on guiding the aircraft to its designated Combat Air Patrol (CAP) area. Changing frequency they soon established contact with the German GCI known as 'Crabtree' and while the pilot was busy navigating the aircraft the navigator in the rear cockpit was unaware that he had made the Master Arm safety switch live.

Around 35 miles (56km) from base the backseater detected a pair of contacts on his radar and the decision was taken to engage the targets. Normally, for the purpose of evaluation, the engagement would be filmed and the 'kill' verified post-flight by looking at the navigator's radar camera. This recorded the target's range and the moment of trigger press by an event marker.

On this occasion, the pilot quickly identified the targets as a pair of RAF SEPECAT Jaguars which had fortuitously pulled up to around 1,000ft (305m) as they approached their base at the end of a mission and were focusing on their recovery checks.

As the Phantom crew started to turn towards the Jaguars, the latter's pilots saw the fighter but being low on fuel they chose not to engage in a dogfight.

However, moments after the pilot of the second of the two Jaguars (XX963/AL) saw Phantom XV422 pass behind his aircraft there was a loud explosion and the Jaguar rapidly lost control. Assuming some sort of catastrophic failure the Jaguar pilot instinctively pulled the lower Martin-Baker ejector seat handle and swiftly found himself in a field 50 miles from base, while his aircraft crashed onto open farmland.

▲ A mixture of camouflage and air defence grey Phantoms in the early 1980s.

◀ Although much attempt was made to hide XV422's unusual claim to fame some members of the RAF felt it important to give the jet special recognition!

What Went Wrong?

The Phantom navigator is adamant that he had pulled the vital CB to render XV422's weapon system inert – but there was a catch. The bank of CBs was located on the right hand wall of the rear cockpit and it is very possible that under 'G' his leg may have been pushed against the wall causing the CB to pop back in.

In fact, after landing XV422 was impounded and the engineers found that the CB was faulty– it only needed to be pushed in slightly and contact was re made.

So how did the pilot forget that he had live missiles? Training was relentless during the Cold War, to such an extent that actions became autonomous.

But what about the cross of white tape applied to Master Arm switch? Shouldn't this have made it impossible to physically squeeze the trigger and fire the missile? It would have done – but for some unknown reason the tape was not applied to XV422.

Finally, the GCI controller was not told the aircraft was 'live armed' and therefore didn't remind the crew to perform this vital check.

At a lengthy and public board of enquiry the blame fell squarely on the crew who had pulled the trigger and achieved the RAF's only air-to-air kill with the mighty FGR2. Both crew were found to be guilty and punished, though both continued to fly fighters.

A breakdown of safety checks led to the pilot getting the 'growl' in his headset, squeezing his trigger... and getting his 'Kill'. ❖

THE LEGACY

Following the incident XV422 became a slight embarrassment to the RAF. After a major overhaul the aircraft found its way back to RAF Germany and was issued to 19(F) Sqn. It was perhaps more than a coincidence that the airframe was coded 'J'. Not ones to miss an opportunity the ground crew soon added to the 'J' and 'Juliet' became 'J.ag Killer'!

With the end of the Cold War the RAF Phantoms were all returned to UK to be issued to either 56 or 74 Sqns or to be scrapped. With some airframe life left on it XV422 joined 56 (F) Sqn but close observation of the airframe revealed some subtle 'zapping' across the fuselage and wings where red 'cat' paw prints had been painted prior to it leaving Germany!

Upon retirement XV422 survived the mass scrapping and was delivered to RAF Stornoway the most remote station in the UK – an unusual location as the F-4 had little association with the base.

Unloved, the aircraft was soon up for disposal and a team from RAF St Athan was sent to scrap it. Under tight US/UK rules the aircraft had to be disposed of thoroughly and preservation groups were discouraged from taking on these Cold War relics. The aviation world has long assumed that the infamous XV422 had vanished without trace – however a chance meeting by the author in 2014 discovered that far from being destroyed some significant parts of her were preserved, a welcome discovery for such an historic airframe.

There is another relic of that fateful day. 92 Sqn salvaged the nose wheel door from Jaguar XX963 and it still hangs proudly in the squadron's crew room to this day – as fighter pilots say – "a Kill's a Kill!"

FLYING COLOURS
RAF Special Schemes

Throughout their career RAF Phantoms have been adorned with some spectacular colour schemes. Here is just a small selection of the some of the most decorative.

When 74 (Tiger) Sqn officially stood down at RAF Wattisham, Suffolk on October 1, 1992 it held a mini 'Tiger Meet' event with aircraft attending from France, Portugal and the USA. To commemorate the event Phantom FGR.2 XV404 was painted in this spectacular 'Tiger' scheme. It was one of the few times a 74 Sqn machine had been so extensively adorned but sadly the aircraft chosen had already been withdrawn from use and could not fly. The unit was the last RAF squadron to operate the Phantom and in early October 1992 it moved to RAF Valley, Anglesey to fly the Hawk as part of 4 FTS. Sadly XV404 did not follow and was scrapped on site. On October 31, 1992 RAF Wattisham stood down as a fighter base. *KEY – Steve Fletcher*

◀ In 1979, to mark the 60th anniversary of Alcock and Brown's first successful non-stop transatlantic crossing, the RAF embarked on a special flight. John Alcock's nephew, Tony, was a Flight Commander with 56(F) Sqn at RAF Wattisham and he convinced the RAF powers-that-be to allow him to paint up a Phantom in special gloss markings and recreate his uncle's famous flight. A search of the Phantom fleet turned up a suitably named navigator and Norman Browne joined him on the trip. The eye-catching and patriotic scheme on XV424 also carried the flags of all the NATO nations (to mark the 30th anniversary of the organisation) and the new generation Alcock and Brown(e) departed Goose Bay, Newfoundland, Canada 60 years to the day after the original Vickers Vimy had done likewise. The flight had taken 5 hours and 40 minutes, almost a third of the 15 hours and 57 minutes it had taken the Vimy! Today XV424 is on show at the RAF Museum, Hendon, although it shed its special scheme shortly after the commemoration. *Crown Copyright*

◀ One of the more 'subdued' special schemes worn by an RAF Phantom was applied to 111 Sqn FGR.2 XV574 in 1989. Dubbed 'Flagship Zulu' the aircraft wore these markings until it was scrapped in 1991. *KEY – Duncan Cubitt*

◀ Among the most distinctive RAF Phantoms were the 'Bluesome Twosome.' The two jets (XT899 and XV408) were painted in this commemorative scheme by 19 Sqn and 92 Sqn respectively and performed the last symbolic 'Battle Flight' over the East/West Germany air defence zone at midnight on October 2/3, 1990. The following day the newly unified Germany took over responsibility for its own air defence. Both jets survive to this day with XT899 retaining its blue scheme while on display in Prague and XV408 on show at the Tangmere Military Aviation Museum, where it has recently regained its blue scheme. *KEY – Duncan Cubitt*

▶ Phantom FG.1 XT597 first flew on November 1, 1966 and spent her entire life on various trials work, including the initial carrier suitability trials on USS *Coral Sea* [see page 30]. In 1974 the jet joined the Aircraft & Armaments Experimental Establishment at Boscombe Down, Wiltshire and was used as a flying laboratory for many years wearing the unit's characteristic red, white and blue 'raspberry ripple' colour scheme. In 1983 the aircraft gained special markings to mark the 25th anniversary of the F-4 Phantom at the International Air Tattoo at RAF Greenham Common. Upon retirement XT597 was donated to the museum at Boscombe Down but in 2012 it was sold to Everett Aero. The aircraft remains for sale at its Bentwaters, Suffolk base. *KEY – Duncan Cubitt*

◀ Perhaps the most famous of all RAF Phantoms was XV582 'Black Mike.' The jet was painted up by 111 Sqn engineers in 1989 to mark the 30th anniversary of the unit's famed Black Arrows display team. In recent years Black Mike has been saved for posterity and a full feature on the aircraft appears on page 60. *KEY – Duncan Cubitt*

Although it did not wear a 'special scheme' as such, Phantom XT914 wore 74 Sqn's Tiger's Head emblem on the tail while serving as the RAF's last solo Phantom display aircraft in 1992. The RAF Wattisham, Suffolk-based aircraft was flown by Archie Liggat and Mark 'Manners' Manwaring and performed a memorable airshow routine at venues across the country. XT914 is seen here bursting a tyre while landing at North Weald, Essex during the annual Fighter Meet Airshow. Today the aircraft is on show at the Wattisham Heritage Museum. *KEY – Duncan Cubitt*

PHANTOM LOSSES

For such a large and complex fighter the Phantom suffered a relatively low attrition rate while in British service. Here we provide an overview of the most notable losses and incidents incurred by Fleet Air Arm and Royal Air Force squadrons

Phantom FG.1 XT861 first flew on March 3, 1968 and was delivered to the Royal Navy on June 18 of the same year. It is seen here at RAF Abingdon, Oxfordshire on September 14, 1973 while being prepared for RAF service. The aircraft was lost on September 7, 1987 following a mid-air collision over the North Sea. The crew ejected safely. *Adrian M Balch*

Date	Variant	Reg	Unit
July 9, 1969	FGR.2	XV395	6 Sqn

Suffered a system failure near Horncastle, Lincolnshire forcing Flt Lts Forbes M Pearson and John E Roome to eject safely.

| May 3, 1970 | FG.1 | XV566 | 892 NAS |

While on loan to the Aircraft & Armaments Experimental Establishment (A&AEE) the aircraft crashed into the sea near Lyme Bay, Dorset. Lts A J Stewart and P J Coombes were both killed.

| May 19, 1971 | FG.1 | XT862 | 767 NAS |

Engines flamed out during a steep climb causing Cdr W Hawley and Lt P Love to eject safely at 5,000ft. The aircraft crashed into the sea 25 miles west of Newquay, Cornwall.

| June 28, 1971 | FG.1 | XV565 | 892 NAS |

Crashed during low-level air combat manoeuvring while flying from Cecil Field AFB, Florida. The jet crashed into the sea off Mayport, Florida and Lts D Hill and M Grainger-Holcombe were picked up by helicopter after ejecting safely.

| October 12, 1971 | FGR.2 | XV479 | 54 Sqn |

Aircraft suffered a reheat failure after take-off from Karup AB, Denmark and was unable to maintain altitude. Flt Lts Richard 'Dick' Northcote and Steve B Cox both ejected safely but the aircraft landed on a cottage killing two civilians.

| October 15, 1971 | FGR.2 | XT904 | 228 OCU |

Lost control during a spin near Cromer, Norfolk. Sqn Ldr John D Armstrong and Flt Lt Miles ejected safely.

| January 10, 1972 | FG.1 | XT876 | 767 NAS |

After suffering a double flame-out while carrying out a supersonic interception at 31,000ft the Phantom entered a spin. Pilot Cmdr Simon Idiens and navigator Lt Rod O'Conner both ejected at 15,000ft but the pilot's parachute malfunctioned and his body was never found. The aircraft crashed into the sea near Trevose Head, Cornwall.

| February 14, 1972 | FGR.2 | XT913 | 228 OCU |

Suffered a hydraulic failure over the North Sea forcing Flying Officer Jack Stine and Flt Lt Lee Preston to eject safely. The jet crashed into the sea one mile north of Happisburgh, Norfolk.

| November 21, 1972 | FGR.2 | XV477 | 6 Sqn |

Aircraft crashed into Scarrowmanwick Fell, nine miles east of Penrith, Cumbria, in deteriorating weather. Flt Lt Christopher Haynes and his navigator Flt Lt Martin Smith did not eject and were killed.

| June 1, 1973 | FGR.2 | XV397 | 17 Sqn |

While flying from RAF Bruggen, Germany the aircraft suffered an instrument failure and inadvertently entered a steep dive in poor visibility. The pilot, Sqn Ldr George Roberts, ejected safely but navigator Flt Lt David Baker was struck by the pilot's canopy and killed.

| June 25, 1973 | FGR.2 | XV440 | 31 Sqn |

Aircraft flew into the sea during night operations off Vlieland in The Netherlands. Pilot Flt Lt Hugh Kennedy and navigator David Dodges were both killed.

| July 25, 1973 | FG.1 | XT871 | 892 NAS |

While taking off from HMS *Ark Royal* the port engine failed and the jet crashed off the bow and into the Firth of Forth near Isle of May, Scotland. Pilot Lt J Gunning ad navigator Lt Rod O'Conner both ejected safely and were picked up by SAR Wessex helicopter.

| August 22, 1973 | FGR.2 | XV427 | 17 Sqn |

Flew into high ground at Arfeld, Bad Berleburg, West Germany killing Flt Lts Keith Spawton and Michael Harris. The aircraft had dropped out of a four-ship formation during a turn and the pilot attempted to re-join by 'cutting a corner' but flew into the surrounding terrain.

| October 15, 1973 | FG.1 | XT869 | 892 NAS |

While landing at RAF Leuchars, Fife the aircraft suffered a complete engine failure and crashed in the Tentsmuir Forest. Lt Hooton and Lt D J Lortscher (USN) ejected safely at 400ft and survived with minor injuries.

PHANTOM LOSSES

August 9, 1974 — FGR.2 — XV493 — 41 Sqn
Collided in mid air with a Piper Pawnee crop-spraying aircraft (G-ASVK) near Downham Market, Norfolk. Pilot Group Captain David Blucke and navigator Flt Lt Terry Kirkland were both killed, as was the crop sprayer Paul Hickmott.

October 11, 1974 — FGR.2 — XV431 — 31 Sqn
Crashed on take-off in West Germany when the wings (which had been left unlocked) folded in flight. Flt Lts Ray Pilley (pilot) and Kevin Toal (navigator) both ejected and survived.

November 21, 1974 — FGR.2 — XV441 — 14 Sqn
While operating from RAF Bruggen, West Germany the aircraft caught fire and crashed near Lang Hent in The Netherlands. Pilot Flt Lt 'Mike' Keane and navigator Flt Lt Ian Vacha both ejected safely.

March 3, 1975 — FGR.2 — XV416 — 111 Sqn
The aircraft suffered an engine failure over the River Witham shortly after taking off from RAF Coningsby, forcing Flt Lts Phil Tolman and P Trotter to eject safely. The jet crashed into the river.

September 18, 1975 — FG.1 — XV580 — 43 Sqn
While undertaking aerobatic practice for an upcoming airshow the aircraft lost control and crashed near Kirriemuir, Scotland. Flying Officer Wright and Flt Lt Jack Hammil both ejected safely.

November 24, 1975 — FGR.2 — XV405 — 228 OCU
Lost during a training flight from RAF Coningsby, Lincolnshire. Flt Lts Smith and Lunn both ejected safely. The aircraft crashed into the sea off Skegness, Lincolnshire.

December 17, 1975 — FGR.2 — XV463 — 41 Sqn
The aircraft crashed into the Solway Firth, Cumbria after a loss of control. Both crew members were killed.

July 23, 1976 — FGR.2 — XV417 — 29 Sqn
During air combat training against a pair of Dutch F-104 Starfighters the aircraft pulled 5G and suffered a structural failure that saw the starboard wingtip fold. The jet crashed near Mablethorpe, Lincolnshire but pilot Flt Lt Jim Jackson and navigator Capt 'Dave' Newberry (RCAF) both ejected safely.

May 18, 1977 — FG.1 — XV588 — 892 NAS
Aircraft caught fire during take-off from RAF Leuchars, Fife. The take-off was abandoned and Flying Officer Newby and Flt Lt Riley safely evacuated the aircraft.

November 21, 1977 — FGR.2 — XV571 — 43 Sqn
During take-off the nosewheel steering locked, forcing the aircraft to run onto the grass at high speed. Flt Lts Steve Gyles and Andy Moir both ejected safely – although the latter broke a leg.

May 12, 1978 — FG.1 — XT868 — 892 Sqn
During a practice for an air display at RAF Leuchars (to mark the last Royal Navy Phantom flight) the aircraft crashed on final approach. The starboard wingtip hit the ground causing the jet to cartwheel. Cdr Carl Davies ejected as the aircraft was on its side but observer Lt John Gavin was unable to vacate the Phantom and died in the accident.

July 24, 1978 — FGR.2 — XV483 — 92 Sqn
During a practice intercept while flying as part of RAF Germany the aircraft flew into the ground near Drenke, West Germany killing Sqn Ldr Chris Cunningham and Flt Lt Chris Meade.

August 4, 1978 — FGR.2 — XV403 — 111 Sqn
Flew into the North Sea east of Aberdeen during a practice interception. The pilot, Capt Josh Tallentyre (USMC), and navigator Flt Lt Chris Ferris were both killed.

November 23, 1978 — FG.1 — XT598 — 111 Sqn
While attempting to land at RAF Leuchars, Fife the aircraft flew into the sea killing Flt Lts Chris Jones and Michael Hardy-Stephenson.

February 28, 1979 — FG.1 — XV578 — 111 Sqn
While undertaking fighter affiliation training against a Vulcan both engines seized causing Sqn Ldr Mal Gleeve and F/O Al Lewry to eject safely 50 miles east of Montrose, Scotland. The aircraft crashed into the North Sea.

March 5, 1980 — FGR.2 — XV436 — 29 Sqn
Missed the arrestor cable during an emergency landing at night at Coningsby, Lincolnshire following hydraulic failure. The crew ejected and the aircraft ran off the runway and into a field.

This Phantom FGR.2 was delivered to the RAF as XV427 on January 25, 1969 and is seen here being operated by A&AEE the following August. It subsequently joined 17 Sqn in Germany but was lost when it flew into high ground on August 22, 1973 killing Flt Lts Keith Spawton and Michael Harris. *Adrian M Balch*

PHANTOM LOSSES

Phantom FG.1 XV580 was lost at RAF Leuchars on September 18, 1975 while practicing aerobatics ahead of the base's Battle of Britain Airshow. *Airspace Images*

June 3, 1980   FGR.2   XV589   29 Sqn
The aircraft crashed while landing at RAF Alconbury, Cambridgeshire after the radome latches failed, causing the radome to open in flight. Flt Lts Pat Watling and Steve James both ejected safely.

July 11, 1980   FGR.2   XV418   92 Sqn
During a filming sortie the aircraft dived into the ground near Diepholz, West Germany. Flt Lts Andrew Mott and Ian Johnson were killed after failing to eject.

November 12, 1980   FGR.2   XV413   29 Sqn
During a night flight the aircraft crashed into the sea 50 miles off the coast of Cromer, Norfolk. Sqn Ldr Stephen Glencorse and navigator Flt Lt Graham Finch were both killed.

December 9, 1980   FGR.2   XV414   23 Sqn
The aircraft suffered an engine fire over the North Sea, ten miles east of Lowerstoft, Suffolk. Flt Lt Steve Martin and his navigator ejected safely.

January 26, 1981   FGR.2   Unknown   TBC
Flt Lts Nick Morgan and Bob Lawley ejected safely after the nosewheel steering locked during take-off.

July 9, 1981   FG.1   XT866   43 Sqn
The aircraft suffered an avionics failure while landing at night at RAF Leuchars, Fife. It subsequently crashed and cartwheeled before catching fire. Sqn Ldr Ray Dixon and F/O R Syndercombe managed to eject and survive.

April 14, 1982   FGR.2   XT912   228 OCU
Suffered a mid-air collision with Phantom XT903 shortly after take-off from RAF Coningsby. XT903 landed safely but XT912 crashed near Walcot, Lincolnshire. Sqn Ldr Dick George and Guy Slocum both ejected successfully.

April 14, 1982   FGR.2   XT903   228 OCU
Suffered a mid-air collision with Phantom XT912 shortly after take-off from RAF Coningsby. XT903 landed safely but XT912 crashed near Walcot, Lincolnshire.

July 7, 1982   FGR.2   XV491   29 Sqn
Crashed into the sea 35 miles east of Cromer, Norfolk killing Flt Lt Alan Stewart and his navigator Flt Lt Marcus Hanton.

October 17, 1983   FGR.2   XV484   23 Sqn
Flew into cloud obscured high ground near Mount Usborne, Falkland Islands killing Flt Lts John Gostick and Jeff Bell.

March 6, 1984   FGR.2   XT891   29 Sqn
While taking off from RAF Waddington the crew were unable to maintain directional stability after XT891's nosewheel steering failed. The aircraft departed the runway and pilot, Flt Lt T J 'Zip' Nolan, and navigator Flt Lt Roger Newton ejected safely. The aircraft was eventually returned to service and is now the Gate Guardian at RAF Coningsby.

August 19, 1984   FG.1   XV569   11 Sqn
While taking off from Bournemouth (Hurn) Airport following an air display the aircraft's nosewheel steering failed. The aircraft veered onto the grass and pilot F/O Dave Harvey hauled it into the air at a high angle of attack. The navigator (Flt Lt Pete Humphreys) safely ejected at low level and the pilot continued with the flight, landing safely at RAF Lyneham 45 minutes later using the emergency arrestor wire.

August 21, 1985   FG.1   XT857   43 Sqn
The aircraft was written off following a heavy landing at RAF Leuchars, Fife.

January 7, 1986   FGR.2   XV434   29 Sqn
Suffered a loss of control while flying at low-level 20 miles north of Harrogate Yorkshire. Flt Lts Ian Ferguson and S C Williams both ejected safely.

July 3, 1986   FGR.2   XV471   19 Sqn
Suffered a major hydraulic failure on approach to RAF Wildenrath, West Germany forcing F/O Russ Waters-Morgan and Flt Lt Chris Heames to eject.

August 26, 1987   F-4J(UK)   ZE358   74 Sqn
During a low-level training flight the aircraft flew into the ground ten miles southwest of Aberystwyth, Wales. Pilot, Flt Lt Euan Murdoch and navigator F/O Jeremy Lindsey did not eject and both were killed.

September 7, 1987   FG.1   XT861   43 Sqn
During a five-ship formation flight over the North Sea XT861 was involved in a mid-air collision with Phantom XT872. The crew of XT861 (F/O John Hancock and Sqn Ldr Rommy Riddell) ejected safely after it pitched up and rolled uncontrollably. The jet crashed into the North Sea 55 miles east of the Tay Estuary, Perthshire. XT872 landed back safely at RAF Leuchars, Fife.

PHANTOM LOSSES

December 31, 1987   FG.1   XV591   111 Sqn
Declared a write-off after a major structural fault was discovered during routine servicing at RAF Leuchars, Fife. The cockpit was painted in the 'Alcock & Brown' colour scheme and used for display purposes at RAF St Athan, Wales before moving to the RAF Museum, Cosford, Shropshire.

April 20, 1988   FG.1   XT860   43 Sqn
The aircraft was involved in Exercise Elder Forest and flew into the sea 28 miles east of RAF Leuchars, Fife killing Ft Lts Philip Clarke and Kevin Poysden.

August 2, 1988   FGR.2   XV501   56 Sqn
Suffered a major systems failure while flying near Mayenne, France and crashed. Flt Lts D Johnson and N Hacke both ejected successfully.

September 23, 1988   FGR.2   XV248   228 OCU
Whilst practising for the following day's Battle of Britain airshow at RAF Abingdon the aircraft failed to recover from an aerobatic manoeuvre and crashed, killing pilot Flt Lt Christopher Lackman and navigator Flt Lt William Thompson.

October 18, 1988   FGR.2   XV437   92 Sqn
The aircraft suffered engine problems near Holzminden, West Germany causing Flt Lts Pete Lynes and Colin Fryer to eject safely from an altitude of 2,000ft.

December 6, 1988   FG.1   XT864   111 Sqn
Tailplane removed from the aircraft when a fuel bowser collided with it at RAF Leuchars, Fife. With the imminent withdrawal of the type it was not repaired and was allocated to 8998M and placed on the gate at Leuchars.

January 9, 1989   FGR.2   XT908   228 OCU
The pilot, Sqn Ldr John Nelson, informed his navigator that he was feeling unwell. Moments later the aircraft dived into the sea 50 miles east of Dundee, Scotland. Navigator Flt Lt Gordon Moulds ejected and was picked up by helicopter.

April 24, 1989   FGR.2   XT893   56 Sqn
Suffered a major systems failure causing the crew to eject 48 miles east of Flamborough Head, Yorkshire. Sqn Ldr Chris J Bagnall and Flt Lt Richard Watson were picked up unharmed by helicopter.

April 1, 1990   FGR.2   XV478   19 Sqn
Badly damaged in a ground fire at Wildenrath, West Germany. Due to the impending retirement of the type it was not repaired

April 30, 1990   FGR.2   XV402   56 Sqn
The port tyre burst during a hard landing at RAF Valley, Anglesey and sparks from the wheel ignited fuel from a ruptured fuel tank. The navigator (Flt Lt S Lungley) ejected but pilot Sqn Ldr G Yapp stayed with the aircraft. The fire was extinguished but it had caused considerable damage to the underside of the aircraft. It was not repaired.

October 9, 1990   FGR.2   XV394   92 Sqn
Damaged in a flying accident at RAF Wildenrath, West Germany. Repairs were halted due to the type's withdrawal and the aircraft was ultimately scrapped.

January 9, 1991   FGR.2   XV462   19 Sqn
The aircraft suffered a loss of control while flying off the coast of Cyprus. Flt Lt Graham Williams and F/O Gary Wainwright ejected safely.

August 12, 1991   FGR.2   XV438   56 Sqn
Collided in mid-air with Phantom XV473. XV438 lost the top of its tail and with the withdrawal of the type it was not repaired.

August 12, 1991   FGR.2   XV473   56 Sqn
Collided in mid-air with Phantom XV438. The aircraft was only slightly damaged and flew again (see also July 15, 1992).

October 30, 1991   FG.1   XV421   1453 Flt
During air combat practice 50 miles north of Stanley, Falkland Islands the aircraft was seen to emerge from low cloud and crash into the sea. The 19 Sqn crew (pilot F/O Ian Halden and navigator Flt Lt Chris Weightman) were killed.

July 15, 1992   FGR.2   XV473   56 Sqn
Made an emergency landing at Waddington, Lincs due to a fuel pump blowing in a wing tank. With the withdrawal of the type from service it was not repaired. It was later destroyed during its first fire training session as the fuel tanks had not been drained beforehand!

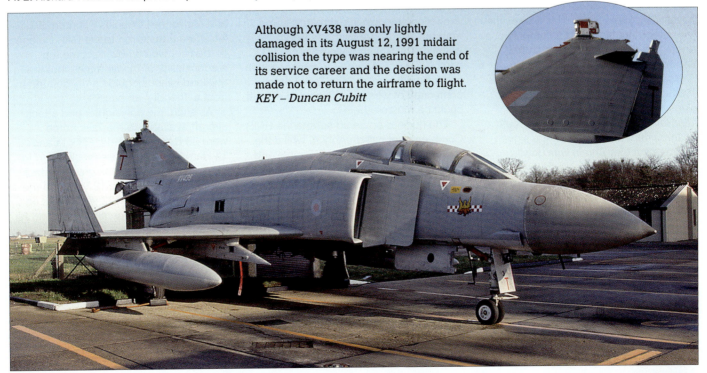

Although XV438 was only lightly damaged in its August 12, 1991 midair collision the type was nearing the end of its service career and the decision was made not to return the airframe to flight.
KEY – Duncan Cubitt

Defending the South Atlantic Falklands Phantoms

Faith (XV472) and *Desperation* (XV466) pose for the camera over typically barren Falkland Island terrain in 1991.
All KEY Collection unless stated

The lack of air defence in the South Atlantic became apparent during the 1982 Falklands War. The Phantom ultimately came to the rescue and continued in the role for almost a decade.

On April 2, 1982, Argentinian military forces did the unthinkable. Despite repeated warnings by Royal Navy captain Nicholas Barker, the Argentine junta launched an amphibious landing on the British outpost in the South Atlantic.

Barker had long campaigned that the 1981 defence review, which included plans to withdraw HMS *Endurance* (the Navy's only presence in the South Atlantic) from the region, sent a signal to Argentina that Britain was unwilling, and would soon be unable to defend its subjects in the Falklands.

Now, early on a Friday morning hoards of military forces were streaming ashore with next to no resistance. It was clear that something had to be done and during an emergency meeting the Chief of the Naval Staff, Admiral Sir Henry Leach, advised Prime Minister Margaret Thatcher that "Britain could and should send a Task Force." This was backed in an emergency session of the House of Commons on April 3 and soon ships were sailing to the region.

Task Force

With the Cold War still raging the RAF, Royal Navy and British Army were expecting any possible threat to come from the East… not from the South Atlantic. The British government was completely unprepared for military action so far from home and the Task Force comprised of whatever ships and aircraft could be mustered.

The nuclear-powered submarine HMS *Conqueror* set sail on April 4, whilst the two aircraft carriers HMS *Invincible* and HMS *Hermes*, in the company of escort vessels, left Portsmouth a day later.

The luxury ocean liners SS *Canberra* and the QE2 were requisitioned and set sail with 3 Commando Brigade and the 5th Infantry Brigade aboard respectively. The entire Task Force eventually comprised 127 ships: 43 Royal Navy vessels, 22 Royal Fleet Auxiliary ships and 62 merchant ships.

However, what was most lacking was a large aircraft carrier capable of launching and recovering heavy interceptor and bomber aircraft. Just four years earlier the British government had announced that HMS *Ark Royal* would be scrapped and her Blackburn Buccaneers and McDonnell Douglas Phantom FG.1 jets were transferred to the RAF. Defence of the fleet would now become the responsibility of the air force – but the Falkland Islands could hardly be further from a 'friendly' air base.

As such, the only fighter and attack aircraft available to the Task Force were 28 BAe Sea Harrier FRS.1s and 14 Harrier GR.3s. These would need to be employed in both the ground attack role and to protect the 127 ships in the fleet from a force of 122 jet fighters on strength with the Argentine Navy and Air Force.

Wideawake

As the fleet steamed south, the RAF had to come up with a plan that would enable it to provide both air cover and ground attack support. The decision was made to relocate Phantom fighters, Avro Vulcan bombers, Handley Page Victor tankers and Hawker Siddeley Nimrod

Most of the flying in the Falklands involved flying low-altitude (often 'ultra-low') intercepts.

reconnaissance aircraft to the Ascension Island's Wideawake Airfield. This may have been the closest friendly airfield to the Falkland Islands – but it was still a staggering 3,956 miles (6,366km) from the island's capital at Port Stanley.

By mid-April the aircraft were in place and soon the main British naval Task Force arrived to prepare for active service. In the meantime, a small force had already been sent south to recapture South Georgia.

While the Vulcans were to famously overfly the Falkland Islands and drop their weapons in anger – and the Nimrods were frequent sights over the contested islands and their surrounding waters – the Phantoms lacked the range to be of any real use and were essentially used to provide air defence of Ascension Island.

It would be the Harriers and Sea Harriers that gave the British forces air superiority over the Falkland Islands and enabled ground and Naval forces to retake the British territory on June 14. By that point 255 members of the British forces had lost their lives and 775 had been wounded. The invaders had lost 649 men with a further 1,657 wounded and 11,313 captured as prisoners of war. Three civilians also lost their lives.

In terms of military hardware, the Task Force lost two destroyers, two frigates and three other ships along with 24 helicopters and ten fighters (plus a Vulcan impounded in Brazil after diverting). Conversely, the aggressors lost one cruiser, one submarine, four cargo ships, two patrol boats and one 'spy' trawler along with 25 helicopters, 35 fighters, two bombers, four cargo aircraft, 25 attack aircraft and nine armed trainers.

XV466 *Desperation* launches on another mission from RAF Mount Pleasant in early 1992.

Aftermath

Although the Argentine ground forces had surrendered the British still faced the problem of potential air attacks from Argentina. It was obvious to all involved that the Falkland Islands desperately needed its own air defence, but the only runway had been badly damaged by Vulcans and Sea Harriers during the conflict and it would be some time before it was capable of supporting operations by fast jets.

Accordingly, an aircraft carrier had to remain on station off the coast to use its Sea Harriers to guard the islands' airspace. HMS *Hermes* was the first

FALKLANDS PHANTOMS

Two 1435 Flight Phantoms overfly Port Stanley airfield during a flight from nearby RAF Mount Pleasant.

Left: At Port Stanley the conditions for the QRA crews were bleak. When RAF Mount Pleasant was opened the aircraft now had more substantial hangars but the facilities were still less than ideal. **Right:** Low over the ocean this pair of 1435 Flight QRA Phantoms make a powerful statement of intent for any nation considering unwanted advances on the British Isles' far flung territory.

to take on the guard duty, whilst HMS *Invincible* went north to change a main engine at sea. *Invincible* then returned until she was relieved by the newly built HMS *Illustrious*, which was quickly rushed south and commissioned during the journey.

Although the runway was eventually repaired, even then it was deemed unsuitable for fast jets. At just 1,200m (4,000ft), attempting to land a Phantom was ill-advised so the decision was made to lay metal matting to extend the useable runway length and five portable arrestor cables were also flown in to help stop the large aircraft.

The first Phantom FGR.2 to arrive was a 29 Sqn machine, which landed at the airfield on October 17, 1982 and three others quickly followed.

The procedure to land on the short runway involved 'popping' the brake 'chute just prior to touching down and applying a small amount of power. If the aircraft missed the arrestor wire the crew needed to apply full reheat immediately to avoid the risk of overrunning the runway. If all went to plan the jet would stop within 183m (600ft)! This was a relatively simple

> **If all went to plan the jet would stop within 600ft!**

exercise in daylight and good weather, but the Phantoms would need to provide a 24/7 'on call' state so crews needed to practise the procedure in the dark and in the windiest of weather.

The Phantom's role in the region was to provide air defence of the Falklands Islands Protection Zone (FIPZ), which extended to a distance of 200 miles (322km) around the islands. All jets assigned to the job were armed with four AIM-9L Sidewinders and four Skyflash missiles as standard as well as the SUU-23 cannon.

By December 1982, 23 Sqn had become the resident Phantom Detachment ('Phandet') and members of the squadron spent four months on 'tour' in the South Atlantic. Flights of Phantoms were rotated through the station and two aircraft were maintained on Quick Reaction Alert (QRA) at ten-minute readiness, 24 hours a day. There were no hardened shelters for the QRA aircraft and the only hangarage available were a number of semi-portable structures. These consisted merely of tubular aluminium frames over which a waterproof covering was stretched to keep out the elements.

These 'hangars' were subject to a wind

Trailing wingtip vortices as it slows down to stay on station with the tanker, Phantom XV466 takes on fuel from a Hercules. Fuelling could take place anywhere between 20,000ft and 250ft over sea or land.

Aerial refuelling was an essential part of operating the Phantom from the Falklands and resident C-130 Hercules were frequently used for the task. Here, *Desperation* receives a top-up from XV213.

speed limit for opening the doors, so the 'Q' aircraft were mainly kept outside in case they needed to scramble when the wind was too strong to open the doors! Three crews were maintained on QRA at any time – two in the 'shed' and one on call in the 'Mess' – the latter initially consisting of a converted cruise ship moored next to the airfield. This was later 'upgraded' to the Coastel, which was essentially a series of shipping containers joined together to create living accommodation for both the Phantom crews and members of the co-resident Harrier squadron that provided daylight air defence and anti-shipping cover. Temperatures on the island rarely rose above 10C and frequently fell below minus 10C and horizontal snow was not unheard of – neither were winds in excess of 100mph.

RAF Mount Pleasant

It soon became clear that operating from Port Stanley's short runway, and in such basic facilities, on a permanent basis was far from ideal and work began to construct a large new RAF station on the island. It would be the centrepiece of considerably strengthened air defences for the Falkland Islands, South Georgia and the South Sandwich Islands and was intended to deter any future Argentine attempts to take the territories by force.

Mount Pleasant, 20 miles (32km) to the west of Stanley, was chosen as the site for the new station and – despite the enormous challenges of getting materials on site – it was officially opened by Prince Andrew (who served in the Falklands War) on May 12, 1985.

When it became fully operational in early 1986 the conditions were far more favourable for both the aircraft and the men and women employed to fly and maintain them. The average 'tour' therefore reduced from the existing four months to around five weeks.

Operating from Mount Pleasant 'normalised' QRA operations and brought them into line with similar operations in the UK and Germany. More permanent Q-Sheds were a boon for ground and air crew alike, although the notoriously strong island gales could still cause problems. If the wind was blowing from the west it was almost impossible to walk through the Q1 shed because of the funnelling effect of the wind. Instead you had to climb over the revetment to reach

1435 Flight Phantoms routinely flew fully armed and were fitted with countermeasures including chaff and flares.

FALKLANDS PHANTOMS

The aircraft from 1435 Flight have traditionally worn a Maltese Cross on their tail. This is in tribute to their strong connection with the island and the RAF's determination to keep the islands of both Malta and the Falklands free from oppression.

Left: *Faith* on a long final approach to land at RAF Mount Pleasant in 1992. The type was resident on the Falkland Islands from October 1982 until July 1992. **Right:** A 1435 Flight Phantom returns to the island after another successful scramble. Initially, crews would spend up to four months on the 'Phandet' to the Falklands, although this was later reduced to around five weeks.

▶ The Typhoon has guarded Falkland Island airspace since 2009. Although the aircraft are unnamed, the tail codes F, H and C on these three jets are a nod towards the original *Faith*, *Hope* and *Charity*. *Crown Copyright*

your aircraft before you could launch – something that had the potential to hamper your ten-minute response time!

1435 Flight

QRA scrambles remained a common occurrence as Argentina retained a strong-held belief that the Falkland Islands and their surrounding seas and airspace rightly belonged to them. The Phantoms were therefore frequently launched to intercept inbound aircraft. These were mostly Argentinian Navy Lockheed Electras and Fokker F-28s but occasionally Boeing 707 ELINT (Electronic Intelligence) aircraft were encountered.

Crews also regularly flew what was referred to as the 'Presence Run.' This involved a high-level transit to the far western edge of the FIPZ to ensure Argentine radar operators picked up their presence – just to remind them of the jets' capabilities.

Phantoms from 23 Sqn also routinely scrambled to escort the visiting British Airways Boeing 747s, Britannia Airways Boeing 767s and RAF Lockheed Tristars which all brought men and supplies to the islands.

Although ostensibly a morale booster, to welcome visitors to the island and show that the resident fighters could protect the 'air-bridge' to the region there was always the possibility that a marauding Argentinian fighter might forge an attack on the inbound aircraft. Thankfully it never happened, but it was

Left: XV472 off the coast in early 1992. The jet was ultimately scrapped at RAF Mount Pleasant and buried on site.
Right: The blue/green seas look almost tropical but the freezing water temperatures off the Falkland coast would be enough to kill in minutes. This was not the place to eject.

Left: The Phantoms of 1435 Flight were finally replaced by the Tornado F.3 in July 1992. Here, *Faith* and *Charity* pose for the publicity camera high above the islands. *Crown Copyright* **Right:** Phantoms from 1435 Flight would routinely intercept and escort inbound aircraft to the island, such as this RAF Tristar.

a very real possibility at times.

The squadron had acquired its first Phantoms on November 1, 1975 while at RAF Coningsby, Lincolnshire and then moved to RAF Wattisham, Suffolk prior to relocating to the Falklands. By 1987 it was operating a fleet of seven Phantoms in the South Atlantic but it was then selected as one of the RAF's first Panavia Tornado F.3 units and the decision was made to return it back to the UK, where it flew from RAF Leeming in Yorkshire.

However, the Falklands still needed an air defence capability and with the imminent departure of 23 Sqn the decision was made to reform the RAF's 1435 Flight.

The unit had originally formed in Malta in December 1941 and operated in the night fighter and, later, fighter-bomber role using Spitfires, Hurricanes and Bristol Beaufighters. By the end of the war it had operated throughout Sicily, Albania, Yugoslavia and it was finally disbanded at Falconara, Italy in 1945.

When 1435 Flight reformed at Mount Pleasant on November 1, 1988 it was equipped with four Phantom FGR.2s and these were soon named *Faith, Hope, Charity* and *Desperation* by the crews – the first three named after the three Gloster Gladiators that, according to legend, defended Malta during World War Two. The fourth aircraft was, aptly, held in reserve. The Flight is justifiably proud of its Maltese heritage and the Phantoms also gained a bold Maltese Cross emblem on the tail. The unit also carries the motto 'Protect the Right' – a direct reference to the Falkland Islands' motto 'Desire the Right.'

The aircraft continued the QRA duties undertaken by the 23 Sqn jets and the now ageing Phantoms would routinely scramble come day or night in some of the worst weather conditions. The Falkland Islands has an unusual weather system that means it can snow during any month of the year, but the Phantom air and groundcrews needed to be able to launch at short notice irrespective of the meteorological conditions.

Nevertheless, by the early 1990s it became obvious that the Phantom was in desperate need of replacement and with the upcoming retirement of the type in Britain the decision was made to convert 1435 Flight onto the Panavia Tornado F.3 in July 1992.

Flying the Phantoms back to Britain was deemed an unnecessary expense so they were broken up by JCB diggers and buried at Mount Pleasant. Just one of the four – XV409/H *Hope* – escaped the scrapping, and this was placed on display at the base as a gate guardian. However, the corrosive sea air was unkind to the airframe and it too eventually found its way to the scrapman – although the nose section was preserved for the island's museum.

The Tornados continued to maintain provide a 365-day, 24-hour alert until September 2009 when they in turn were replaced by the latest Eurofighter Typhoon FGR.4 jets.

Although the current island guardians do not carry the names *Faith, Hope, Charity* and *Desperation* a subtle reference to their heritage comes in the form of their tail codes – F, H, C and D.

Phantom vs
Classics in Combat

Briefly, in 1992, pilots had the opportunity to test the RAF's incoming and outgoing air defence fighters in mock combat. Tests proved there was still life left in the old Phantom, if it was well flown by a determined crew. *Crown Copyright*

The RAF Phantom fleet was ultimately replaced by the Panavia Tornado F.3 in the early 1990s. Not only was Ian Black privileged to fly both types – he's one of the few people to have dogfighted against an RAF Phantom in an RAF Tornado. He explains how he fared…

The date is July 15, 1992 and in the post Gulf War era the RAF's Phantom fleet is nearing the end of its life. Although still immensely popular with its crews the 'Toom's' days are numbered and the RAF is down to just two operational units: 56 and 74 Sqns – both based at RAF Wattisham in Suffolk.

The UK Air Defence Re-equipment Programme is almost complete and the ageing Avro Shackletons have long gone, as have the last of the single-seat English Electric Lightnings. This is the dawn of a new era where Boeing E-3A Sentry AWACS aircraft now rule the skies and are fully integrated with the Tornado F.3 force.

The Tornado's origins as a low-level bomber are clear to see but under the skin the F.3 is a different beast. It's a two-crew, swing-wing aircraft and carries a war load of air-to-air weaponry almost identical to the old F-4 Phantom's.

The RAF had stuck with the standard combination of four AIM-9Ls and four Skyflash missiles alongside a single gun. On the Tornado F.3 this was a superbly accurate 27mm Mauser cannon neatly fitted into the right hand side of the forward fuselage. This was a major improvement over the Phantom FGR.2 where the UK had purchased 'off the shelf' Phantoms from McDonnell Douglas but, in true Savile Row style, decided to have a few minor alterations. Among the changes was the deletion of the Phantom's internal Vulcan cannon, a decision that led to the RAF hanging a SUU-23 Gatling Gun on the valuable centre-line pylon.

Gunslinger

Some have suggested that the various changes made to the basic Phantom airframe resulted in the bespoke British examples costing five times that of their US brethren. Whether that is true or not it did result in the aircraft having a number of different strengths and weaknesses.

The SU-23 was a formidable weapon in both the air-to-air and air-to-ground roles, but it had some major limitations.

As it was hung under the fuselage – rather than being internally mounted – it created a lot of drag. This meant adding the two outboard 'Fletcher' tanks onto the wings to boost the Phantom's range. This, again, resulted in the loss of two more weapons' hardpoints.

Each time it was fitted to the airframe the gun needed to undergo a lengthy harmonisation procedure. This involved groundcrew spending long hours in the hangar aligning the gun with the aircraft gunsight – any minor alignment issues meant bullets would not hit the target.

However, the gun's mounting system meant it was prone to movement during firm landings and the weapon could need realigning on a regular basis. The Tornado suffered none of these issues with its internal gun.

Back Seater

The biggest difference in the two fighters was to be found in the rear cockpit. The Phantom FGR.2 was a throwback to the 1960s and the back seater had three main tactical displays – Radar, RWR (Radar Warning Receiver) and INAS (inertial navigation and attack system). Using these three devices he controlled the intercept and put the pilot into a firing position.

The RWR was essential for detecting

Tornado

threats and providing the 'air picture' and in a wartime environment the venerable INAS was all he had to navigate with.

Compare this to the post Gulf War Tornado F.3. Now equipped with modern jam-resistant radios, an IFF interrogator and RHWR (Radar Homing Warning Receiver) the avionics 'fit' was far superior to the Phantom (in fact it was also superior to the GR.1 bomber version of the Tornado). The F.3 was also fitted with a pair of superb TV 'tabs', which depicted a plan display along with radar information and, crucially, TWS (Track Whilst Scan).

The Tornado back seater was literally overloaded with information. As conflicts had evolved it was clear that any modern air battle would need a 'battle manager' and in this role the back seater could control his aircraft (or formation) in close link with the AWACS. Crucially he could also guide his pilot around missile engagement zones and remain inside designated kill boxes.

Additionally, modern air defence tactics now relied on a procedure known as 'Bullseye.' This involved picking a common reference point – for example a geographical position of 55 North and 1-degree west. All calls were made relative to that position so that the various crews could build air picture using a common reference point – something that was essential in a big air battle.

The Phantom navigator had to mentally try to work out his own position and then give information relative to that; it was a real art and not at all easy. With the arrival of the Tornado the back seater now had the facility to insert a Bullseye point, thus making his life a whole lot simpler.

perceived threat and how to train for an unknown foe. Admittedly the role of QRA and the defence of UK airspace hadn't changed but the Cold War threat of rushing around West Germany attacking hordes of Warsaw Pact fighters and bombers clearly had.

The first Gulf War was a wake-up call

> **The opportunity now existed for both squadrons to dream up scenarios where each side could use their aircraft to replicate various possible adversaries**

From Front Line to Mud Moving

Air Defence squadrons in the early 1990s had two main tasks: a peacetime training role of defending UK airspace and a wartime role that encompassed the defence of the UK as well as providing fighter escort or sweep to ground attack 'mud moving' packages.

Escort sorties embedded the fighters into (or around) the mud mover's package whereas crews employed on 'sweep' missions would use their fighters ahead of the ground attack package and hopefully sanitise the airspace prior to any large raids.

As the Cold War thawed the RAF was turned upside down in terms of the

for the RAF in terms of how it needed to consider a range of global threats. The Tornado was the RAF's newest fighter and had rightly been pushed to the front line. Not to be outdone, the RAF Phantom force deployed to RAF Akrotiri in Cyprus to defend what was Britain's most valuable asset in the Middle East.

Tornado vs Phantom

In the post Cold War era training no longer looked at an exclusively Soviet threat but considered the possibility that any air force around the globe might be a threat.

With the end of the Phantom force imminent, crews were keen to use up

CLASSICS IN COMBAT

By the early 1990s the UK Air Defence Re-equipment Programme was almost complete with the ageing Avro Shackletons handing over to the Boeing E-3D Sentry AWACS aircraft and Tornado F.3s in the primary air defence role. *Crown Copyright*

every scrap of airframe fatigue left on the old jets. Groundcrew at 56 (F) Sqn were quick to strip the aircraft down to a clean wing configuration and the unit's aircrew were even keener to indulge in some 'proper' combat. The Tornado F.3 normally flew in a clean wing so both jets were now in a similar fit – and soon the opportunity presented itself for the two jets to go head-to-head during some serious training.

At the time, I was based at RAF Leeming with 11(F) Sqn and our Tornado F.3s were all in the capable post-Gulf War modification state. The opportunity now existed for both squadrons to dream up scenarios where each side could use their aircraft to replicate various possible adversaries.

As already discussed, the Phantom and Tornado F.3 bore almost identical weapon loads and in terms of capability were reasonably evenly matched. As most Tornado crews had previously flown the Phantom they had a distinct advantage in that we were acutely aware of the F-4's strengths and limitations.

Against the Phantom the F.3 was in a different league. Although often maligned, the Air Defence Tornado was actually reasonably agile below 10,000ft (3,048m) and it had variable geometry wing sweep affording it both excellent high-speed performance and low speed manoeuvrability. In forward sweep it could

Heavily armed, long-legged and rugged – the Phantom still had a lot going for it despite nearly two decades of service. However, the addition of a centerline gun pod created a lot of drag and meant adding the two outboard 'Fletcher' tanks onto the wings to boost the Phantom's range. This resulted in the loss of three weapons hardpoints. *KEY Collection*

hold its own against a Hawk at low-level – and its two Turbo Union RB199 engines in full reheat and manoeuvre flap made up for most eventualities!

Sadly, the FGR.2 never adopted the leading edge slats that most later F-4s had and the so-called 'hard wing' Phantom was not great at turning – despite what you saw at airshows!

Phantom Aggressors

Prior to each mission the lead crews would have a telephone conversation to see how they would like the sortie to pan out. The trip could either consist of each type being flown in its intended role – or the more complex scenario where one would play the 'aggressor.' The Phantom FGR.2 was not dissimilar in performance

At low-level, and with its wings swept forward the Tornado F.3 could hold its own against a Hawk. *Crown Copyright*

to the Soviet Mikoyan Gurevich MiG-23 *Flogger*, however ordinary squadron pilots were not trained to the same level as USAF Aggressor pilots.

It takes a huge amount of discipline to try to fly your aircraft to replicate a different type – let alone try to utilise the weapons systems to replicate Soviet missiles such as the *Atoll* or *Aphid* missiles. To that end, crews would normally brief missions as 'full up' – with the F.3 and FGR.2 flying with a full weapon fit of four BAe Skyflash missiles, four Sidewinder missiles and a gun, with the option of chaff or flares.

This crews would optimise their war tactics so that the primary weapon of engagement would be the Skyflash. On the Phantom, this had a maximum range at altitude of 20 miles (32km) but the scenario could be made more complex by altering the rules of engagement. A positive hostile identification from the Phantom would mean that he would have to obtain visual contact with the target and identify it as hostile prior to missile release – realistically this would be around 10 miles (16km) from an F-4, even with its optical sight. This was probably too late to avoid a missile shot from the F.3. The Phantom crews would therefore develop highly complex manoeuvres to get into a visual firing position and hope they remained unseen on the Tornado.

With so much fatigue life available the Phantoms could turn tightly without fear of pulling too hard and using up excess airframe hours. Therefore the Phantom boys' preferred choice of scenario was to limit each crew to using just 'Heaters' (Sidewinders), which in turn led to tactics altering as crews now needed to be in visual contact with each other before shooting. It was almost the sport of kings!

Left: The Tornado may have been a modern swing-wing aircraft but it carried almost the same war load of air-to-air weaponry as the old F-4 Phantom. Right: The Tornado F.3 was the RAF's newest fighter and was rightly pushed to the front line during the first Gulf War. *Both pictures Crown Copyright*

CLASSICS IN COMBAT

Left: By 1992 the RAF's Phantom fleet was nearing the end of its life and the service was down to just two operational units: 56 and 74 Sqns – both based at RAF Wattisham in Suffolk. *KEY Collection* **Right:** Demonstrating its clean wing configuration a 56 Sqn Phantom taxies in after a sortie. *KEY Collection*

Groundcrew at 56 (F) Sqn were quick to strip the soon to be retired Phantoms down to a clean wing configuration and the unit's aircrew were even keener to indulge in some 'proper' combat. *KEY Collection*

The Phantom was easy to spot in combat – not just because of its smoky engines but because the Firebirds' 56 Sqn Phantoms had bright red tails! *KEY Collection*

This now meant getting four Phantoms and four Tornados in a very small piece of sky. Trying to engineer a 'turning fight', each formation would brief their tactics to arrive at the 'merge' as fast as possible to avoid any head-on shots but keep the engines as cool as possible. This was essential to avoid the opposition achieving a pre merge head on shot.

Both aircraft were relatively easy to spot in a fight and the red tail fins on the 56 Sqn 'Firebirds' Phantoms certainly helped in that respect.

In terms of self-defence the RAF was slow to adopt the use of infrared decoys and as a cost saving measure rarely used them in training. The Phantom FGR.2 adopted a retrospective system of chaff and flare dispensers behind the sidewinder launch platforms.

Having started with a 'Four vs Four Heaters Only' sortie, the next progression would have been a 'Four vs Four Guns Only' contest – simulating both types armed with a single gun. However, after some close shaves this was never attempted – as trying to get eight aircraft within 350 yards (320m) of each other to shoot the gun was deemed too dangerous!

Four vs Four

Our training area for these final combats was over the Wash just off the North Norfolk coast; an area that allowed us to go supersonic whilst over the sea.

Each formation would brief around two hours prior to take-off and allow 30 minutes to walk to the aircraft and get airborne. Both types could be airborne during wartime in around five minutes but in peacetime things were done at a more leisurely pace.

The brief would cover every aspect of the sortie including the safety aspects – eight high performance fighters in a small space of sky needed careful briefing as the potential for loss of control or mid-air collisions was high.

Limiting our respective weapon loads to just Sidewinders meant the maximum range to achieve a kill would be around 5 miles (8km) and the minimum down to just half a mile (0.8km). This meant there would be lots of close in fights – or 'knife fights in telephone boxes' in fighter pilot parlance.

A crucial part of the brief would be how we would maintain realism by performing 'kill removal.' With both types working different radio frequencies, kills would be passed by ground control interceptors (GCI) to allow the 'dead' to be removed from the fight. The fight would continue until the leader on either side called 'knock it off' – before regrouping for another fight. With both types flying clean wing (without wing tanks) we would be lucky to get two or three engagements done per sortie.

Going Defensive

So, having described the types' respective strengths and weaknesses how did the combat turn out?

From a pilot's perspective the Phantom gave few indications as to its energy levels, something that was vital in the visual engagement. Conversely, the Tornado displayed several visual clues that gave away its energy, most notably its wing sweep position. Above 4G the Tornado also tended to leave distinct vapour trails and the selecting and deselecting of reheat caused a purging of fuel lines and a telltale puff of vapour.

As expected, the Tornado formations had a much better air picture prior to the merge – this despite the F-4 crews trying to perform aggressive manoeuvres prior to the merge to destroy our situational awareness.

Once engaged it was perhaps the biggest 'fur ball' I've witnessed – the Phantom crews were extremely confident with their mounts, despite their handling limitations and the fact that FGR.2 pilots had to use large amounts of rudder to turn the aircraft while simultaneously being careful not to turn and pull whilst loaded at low speed for fear of the aircraft 'departing' from controlled flight.

In comparison, the Tornado had true

A 56 Sqn Phantom pulls hard over the sea during air combat training. *KEY Collection*

A pair of 74 Sqn Phantoms await their next sortie.

In turn 56 Sqn would trade in its Phantoms for the new Tornado F.3 in late 1992. *Crown Copyright*

The changing of the guard – the Phantom handed over responsibility for UK air defence to the Tornado F.3. But in 1992 the chance could not be missed to pit one against the other over the Norfolk coast. *Crown Copyright*

Crews would normally brief missions as 'full up' – with the F.3 and FGR.2 flying with a full weapons fit of four Bae Skyflash missiles, four Sidewinder missiles and a gun, with the option of chaff or flares. In terms of self-defence the RAF was slow to adopt the use of infrared flare decoys and as a cost-saving measure rarely used them in training. *Crown Copyright*

carefree handling and could be flown to the limit at low speeds. At the first merge the result was three kills to the Tornado F.3 and just one to the Phantom.

The second and final merge was more memorable. Flying in an 'extended card' formation as the lead element we started a rapid descent 10 miles (16km) ahead of the Phantoms. In turn, they remained as two units and began engaging our rear element.

With the F.3's excellent cockpit displays we were able to communicate within the formation and knew they were now some 5 miles (8km) south of the fight and we were able to fly in and pick off two FGR.2s from behind.

Sadly, by this point, they had already called two shots on Tornados 3 and 4 – so now it was a down to a classic two vs two dogfight.

The dead guys 'bugged out' and held away from the area as we continued the fight, trying to drag the Phantoms down low and use our superior turn performance. The latter worked well for the first 360 degrees of turn and as I climbed back to 10,000ft (3,048m) to regain energy I could see my wingman was engaged with a single Phantom in a neutral fight. We were now split into two separate one vs one engagements and trying to keep a mental picture of where we all were whilst trying to survive. By the time I reached 10,000ft (3,048m) my adversary was still at 5,000ft (1,524m) over the sea. I could see he was in full reheat and gaining speed.

Sometimes in aviation you have one of those 'time freeze' moments and split seconds of combat stay with you forever. Assuming I was in a good position I rolled my F.3 onto the FGR.2 and started to pull as hard as I could – he did the reverse and pulled hard up into me – I could see him through my Head Up display – a luxury the F-4 didn't have – and tried to get a Sidewinder shot at him face on.

I knew I was too close and the missile wouldn't have time to arm – a big mistake as I wasted valuable seconds trying to get my missile kill whilst the F-4 grew bigger in my windscreen I was now in the vertical (downwards!) accelerating as he was in the vertical heading straight up! Then the penny dropped that we were now pretty much on a collision course and I could see the Phantom pilot wasn't going to give in…

I pushed as hard as I could and hit the front stops with the column as a fire breathing FGR.2 screamed past me in full reheat calling "Fox 3" – the terminology for a guns kills. It was a gutsy move – I'd just been shot in the face by a Phantom as I was pretty much in a vertical dive!

Out of fuel, I called a 'knock it off' and we returned to base. That day, July 15, 1992, I'd tried for too long to get a missile kill whilst the Phantom pilot was hell bent on getting his kill by any means – there was still life in the old dog yet… ❖

Phantom Phase Out — The Axeman Cometh

Twenty-five years ago – in October 1992 – the British military finally said farewell to its frontline Phantoms. It was a sad ending to a career that had spanned three decades.

Even though the RAF had acquired the surplus Royal Navy Phantom FG.1 airframes in the late 1970s the decision to permanently base a squadron of Phantoms on the Falkland Islands [see page 76] in 1982 led to a marked shortage of aircraft to fulfil air defence commitments in the UK and Germany.

With the Cold War at its zenith, replacement airframes or an alternative aircraft were needed urgently. The long-awaited Panavia Tornado F.3 was still some time away from delivery and the RAF needed a stop-gap fighter with a five-year lifespan. Thought was initially, albeit briefly, given to acquiring F-15A Eagles or F-14A Tomcats from the USA. However, common sense eventually prevailed and the decision was made to buy 15 former US Navy F-4J Phantoms for a total of £125 million, including full support.

The jets were refurbished and fitted with 'zero-houred' J79-GE-10B engines with smokeless exhausts. Dubbed the F-4J(UK), the aircraft were also equipped with fatigue life-extending modifications and features including anti-skid brakes before being ferried to the UK in late 1984 and early 1985.

Although they bore little commonality with the F-4K and F-4M that had been ordered as bespoke aircraft for the Royal Navy and RAF respectively, the F-4J(UK) airframes found favour with both air and ground crews. By this point many of the earlier British Phantoms were restricted to 3G when carrying stores, so the new 're-lifed' jets gave pilots the chance to wring the best out of their machines. The 'J' also had superb high-altitude performance and could easily reach 60,000ft (18,288m).

But no matter how loved the jets were, they had been purchased with a proposed five-year lifespan and, true to its word, the MoD began to look at retiring this capable aircraft in 1990. The cost of maintaining what was deemed a 'non-standard' Phantom (which is ironic considering the 'J' models were the most 'standard' Phantoms in British service when compared to the vastly modified, Spey-engined 'K' and 'M' models) was becoming prohibitively expensive and with a worsening spares situation, the decision was made to standardise both 56 'Firebird' Sqn and 74 'Tiger' Sqns on the FGR.2 variant.

The relaxing of rules saw the aircraft belonging to 56 'Firebird' Sqn gain bright red tail fins in their final year of operation and the jets also adopted prominent tail letters that – if lined up correctly – read P H O E N I X and F T R S. Following suit, the jets of 74 'Tiger' Sqn gained black fins, complete with tiger stripes and the tail letters T I G E R and S Q N.
All KEY Collection unless stated

Scrapped

Of the original 15 F-4J(UK)s purchased, a dozen remained in use (ZE355 and ZE362 were in store at St Athan and ZE358 was lost in a fatal accident on August 26, 1987). The surviving aircraft were to be scrapped in 1991 and, somewhat ironically, a farewell flypast of nine of the jets took place on the opening day of the first Gulf War. Many of the aircraft had large amounts of flying hours remaining and could have been of great use to the RAF in a time of conflict, but instead they were ferried to other bases and scrapped.

While the aircraft could arguably have soldiered on for some time yet the Conventional Armed Forces in Europe Treaty, signed in Paris in November 1990, sounded the death knell of not just the 'J' model, but also the entire British Phantom fleet.

The treaty was negotiated during the last years of the Cold War and established limits on key categories of conventional military equipment in Europe. It also mandated the destruction of 'excess weaponry' in the hands of both NATO and Warsaw Pact nations.

Added into this was the fact that the USA had stipulated that US-produced aircraft – even those purchased by UK taxpayers and assembled in the UK from parts largely manufactured by British companies – could not be disposed of to 'non-government' organisations. Thus, requests from private collectors and small museums to preserve Phantoms were almost universally rejected and the majority of the airframes would ultimately succumb to the scrapman's torch.

Meanwhile, back at Wattisham, Suffolk 74 Sqn received a batch of 14 former 228 OCU FGR.2s in January 1991 to bring it into line with 56 Sqn, which had operated that variant for some time.

> **" The Phantom would have been subjected to a major overhaul "**

PHANTOM PHASE OUT

The Tornado F.3 eventually joined the RAF in 1987. By then the E-3 Sentry was replacing the Avro Shackleton in the Airborne Early Warning role but the Phantom would soldier on for another five years. *Crown Copyright*

Phantom crews examine a towed banner following an air to air gunnery session during APC in Cyprus.

With its Speys in full burner a heavily loaded Phantom launches on another sortie from RAF Wattisham.

The centreline SUU-23 gun pod housed the Phantom's six-barrelled M61 Vulcan gatling gun.

FGR.2s from 56 and 74 Sqn line up in the Cyprus sun in 1992 during the final Phantom APC at RAF Akrotiri.

By then the UK Phantom force had been reduced to just four squadrons, however 92 Sqn was to disband in July with 19 Sqn following suit in January 1992. The RAF's 23 Sqn had already traded the type in for new Tornados in 1988, while 43 Sqn followed a year later and 111 Sqn went the same way in 1990. This soon left just 56 and 74 Sqns as the RAF's final Phantom operators.

Multinational Replacement

By the time the Wattisham units were standardising on the FGR.2, the Phantom's replacement in the air defence role had actually been in service for more than five years.

The Panavia Tornado F.3 had begun life as the Tornado ADV (Air Defence Variant) based on the successful ground attack aircraft. Panavia was an international collaboration between the UK, West Germany and Italy and the original Tornado IDS (Interdictor/Strike) had stemmed from a requirement for a multi role combat aircraft (MRCA) in the 1970s. The IDS version of the variable geometry winged aircraft first flew in August 1974 but the ADV interceptor would not fly until more than five years later, on October 28, 1979.

With a powerful Foxhunter radar in its extended fuselage the ADV was designed to combat high-flying soviet bombers and was, in effect, created as a replacement for both the Lightning and Phantom in RAF service. However, delays meant the first Tornado F.2 did not reach squadron service until May 1985 and the definitive F.3 variant was not ready until 1987.

The Lightning fleet was now approaching 30 years of age and in 1988 the type was finally retired from RAF service, but with the Tornado F.3 suffering teething problems the Phantom soldiered on for a few more years.

Throughout this time some serious thought had been given to upgrading the Phantom FGR.2 fleet, so as to provide a

Groundcrew load ammunition for the Phantom's M61 Vulcan cannon during the 1992 APC at RAF Akrotiri.

56 Sqn FGR.2 XT903 taxies in at RAF Akrotiri at the end of the ferry flight from RAF Wattisham.

A pair of 74 Sqn Phantom FGR.2s taxi in at RAF Akrotiri during the now-famous 1992 APC.

backup in case the Tornado programme continued to cause woes. The Phantom would have been subjected to a major overhaul to include a single-piece windscreen, a digital inertial navigation system and an updated radar warning receiver. Other avionics and radar improvements were planned – along with new outer wings to be built by BAe Systems – but a combination of government defence cuts and the sudden turnaround in the ADV programme meant the project was scrapped.

The Tornado F.3 made its combat debut in the 1991 Gulf War when 18 aircraft deployed to Dhahran, Saudi Arabia and, with the problems ironed out, it soon made a name for itself.

Meanwhile, the RAF Phantom fleet was put to work defending British bases on the island of Cyprus during the conflict, thus freeing up Tornados to fly south to defend Saudi Arabia.

Armament Practice Camp

As it happened, the Phantom force was already accustomed to operating from Cyprus as crews had routinely deployed to RAF Akrotiri once a year since 1978 for the annual Armament Practice Camp (APC).

This gave the pilots and navigators the chance to fire live weapons on the ranges and provided a good opportunity for the groundcrew to familiarise themselves with the munitions carried by the jet, most notably the centreline SUU-23 gunpod. A typical APC lasted between six and eight weeks, depending on the number of crews that had to be signed off as qualified.

Crews would practise their gunfire against a large banner towed behind a 100 Sqn Canberra TT.18 target tug but as the Phantoms were normally flown without external tanks each sortie could be as short as 15 minutes. There would typically be four targets flown each day with between four and six aircraft 'attacking' each banner.

PHANTOM PHASE OUT

To mark the imminent retirement of the type Sir John drew together a mixture of 56 and 74 Sqn aircraft to create a truly memorable 'Diamond 16' formation, which he led over Buckingham Palace in June 1992 to mark the Queen's birthday.

Even in the latter years of the type's RAF service both 56 and 74 Sqns deployed to Akrotiri each year for the APC – often with great rivalry showing through. It was no exception in June 1992 when the jets made their final visit to the island. During the now legendary deployment – where many of the photographs illustrating this article were taken – 56 Sqn managed to fly a staggering 56 sorties in a single day. Not to be outdone, 74 Sqn set a goal of flying 74 trips. With just ten jets at its disposal this meant saving time at every possibility – even the brake 'chutes were not jettisoned after landing, rather they were towed back to dispersal so they could be quickly repacked while the jet was being refuelled. By the end of the day the Tigers had achieved their goal – one can only assume the beers were on the Firebird Squadron boys in the bar that evening!

In order to speed up turnarounds during the highly competitive 1992 APC, crews from 74 Sqn dragged their brake 'chutes back to the dispersal so no time was wasted in retrieving them. They would then be repacked while the aircraft was being refuelled and rearmed.

Final Year

The gradual phasing out of the Phantom fleet from the early 1990s meant that 228 Operational Conversion Unit (OCU)'s duties rapidly dwindled as there was no need to train new crews to fly and fight in the ageing aircraft. On January 31, 1991 the unit was officially disbanded and 74 Sqn established a small conversion section for pilots needing to be retrained or refreshed on type.

However, it soon became clear that the following year would finally mark the end of the Phantom's British service career. With such a dedicated following everybody involved with the type was determined that the aircraft would 'go out in style' – and that's exactly what happened.

The relaxing of rules saw the aircraft belonging to 56 'Firebird' Sqn gaining bright red tail fins in their final year of operation and the jets also adopted prominent tail letters that – if lined up correctly – read P H O E N I X and F T R S.

Following suit the jets of 74 'Tiger' Sqn gained black fins, complete with tiger stripes and the tail letters T I G E R and S Q N.

Display Crew

The Phantom had long been a favourite with airshow-goers and bosses at 74 Sqn wanted to ensure that the aircraft made a fitting and memorable finale during the 1992 season.

Seasoned pilot Archie Liggat and navigator Mark Manwaring were chosen

One of the 1992 display Phantoms. The aircraft were selected because of their relatively low fatigue life and general serviceability record.

Fifteen examples of the F-4J(UK) were acquired as a stopgap fighter to serve until the arrival of the Tornado F.3. The variant was the first of the British Phantoms to be completely retired.

Seasoned pilot Archie Liggat and navigator Mark Manwaring were chosen as the final display crew and their enthusiastic solo aerobatic routine was in great demand during the 1992 airshow season.

"The fleet was put to work defending British bases on the island of Cyprus"

as the final display crew and their enthusiastic solo aerobatic routine was in great demand at events across the UK.

The chosen jets had been selected because of their relatively low airframe hours and general levels of serviceability but the season did not go without hitch. On one occasion the Phantom landed heavily at North Weald amidst a cloud of tyre smoke and on another a section of outer wing departed the aircraft mid-display. Unaware of the problem the crew continued their display and landed without issue – such was the durability of the big fighter.

By the end of the 1992 airshow season the pair had flown more than 25 displays and culminated with the RAF's last ever solo Phantom display at Leuchars, Fife on September 19.

Long before the end of the year the cull of excess Phantom airframes began at RAF Wattisham. Within full sight of the 56 Sqn dispersal, surplus FG.1 and FGR.2s gradually met their end as the scrapman arrived on site with either JCB diggers or oxyacetylene torches and began to dismember the once proud aircraft.

Despite the rapid wind-down of the fleet, sufficient airframes were left airworthy for 74 Sqn to fly a dramatic

PHANTOM PHASE OUT

Congratulations Sir! Another APC record is broken.

"That's all folk!" A 74 Sqn crew wave to the crowd as they taxi in from their 'Phinal Phantom Phlight.'

A forlorn trio of Phantoms await their fate at RAF Wattisham in 1992. Nearest the camera is XV439, which was delivered in 1969 and is seen in the markings of its final operator – 92 Sqn

'Diamond Nine' formation in January and in June 56 Sqn mounted an equally impressive nine-ship formation. But in the summer of 1992 it was to be the then AOC, Sir John Allison, who led the most dramatic and famous of all Phantom formations. To mark the imminent retirement of the type Sir John drew together a mixture of 56 and 74 Sqn aircraft to create a truly memorable 'Diamond 16' formation, which he then proceeded to lead over Buckingham Palace to mark the Queen's birthday.

Just days later 56 Sqn finally gave up Phantom operations and moved to RAF Coningsby to become the Tornado F.3 OCU but its counterparts at 74 Sqn would carry on campaigning the Phantom for a few more weeks – and remained operational until the very end.

In early September the RAF's own Tiger Squadron hosted a mini Tiger Meet at Wattisham, inviting aircraft from other 'Tiger' squadrons from around the globe. The opportunity was taken to paint one of its grounded Phantoms (XV404) into a flamboyant tiger scheme, complete with wrap-around black and orange stripes [Ed: see page 70].

Over September 29–30 the remaining Phantoms took part in the Anglo-French Exercise *ARC* and then – just a day later – the base was officially stood down. A ceremonial flypast was flown and then Wattisham fell silent. Later that month the base officially closed and in March 1993 it was handed over to the Army.

Blue Cross

The terms of the Conventional Armed Forces in Europe Treaty meant that each side retained the right to check that the other was actually disposing of the aircraft it claimed to be. The newly retired Phantoms were therefore adorned with large blue crosses – to let any passing Soviet satellites know they were decommissioned. They were then towed across the airfield and broken up in full view of the world.

It was an ignominious end to an aircraft that had served the nation well across three decades. A few survivors [see page 96] managed to escape the clutches of the arms treaty, and America's desire for total scrappage, but for the majority of the jets the end was swift.

> **Everybody involved with the type was determined that the aircraft would 'go out in style'**

The Phantom never fired a single shot in anger during its career with the British forces but it acted as a useful deterrent during the darkest days of the Cold War.

Twenty-five years later the type is remembered fondly by aircrew, groundcrew and enthusiasts alike. It really was a Phantom Phenomenon.

X marks the spot! The Phantoms were adorned with large blue crosses so as to indicate to inquisitive Soviet spy satellite that the aircraft were retired and awaiting destruction.

XT902 on the dump at Wattisham ahead of being scrapped in 1992.

Not even the 'Tiger' schemed XV404 escaped the scrapman's axe.

Not all Phantoms were scrapped immediately. Some had a drawn out 'death' on the fire training grounds at airfields around the country.

XV439 reflects on its past career as it awaits its appointment with the oxyacetylene torch.

THE SURVIVORS

Of the 170 Phantoms flown by the UK military just a handful remain into the 21st century. Here we present a breakdown of the lucky few survivors.

XV586 first flew in 1969 and was delivered to the Royal Navy two months later. It served with 892 NAS on HMS *Ark Royal* until April 1977 when it joined 43(F) Sqn at RAF Leuchars. It retired in 1989 and was placed on gate guard duties at the base. When Leuchars closed the aeroplane was sold and is now preserved at RNAS Yeovilton, Somerset in her original 892 NAS markings.

At the height of the Cold War there were six operational squadrons of Phantoms plus the Operational Conversion Unit. A total of 170 airframes were delivered to the British armed forces (comprising 52 F4K FG.1s and 118 F4M FGR.2s) but the Phantom did not fare well after its retirement.

Unlike some types, such as the Lightning and Vulcan, which were disposed of to museums and private concerns at the end of their military usefulness, the Phantom fleet was mostly scrapped. This was mostly due to post Cold War treaties dictating that aircraft should be broken up and rendered unflyable. This prohibited the sale to museums and certainly prevented any attempts to keep the type flying in private hands. Nonetheless, a small number did manage to escape into civilian ownership, even after MoD efforts to put a stop to some sales after they had gone through. As recently as 2000 the MoD threatened a mass 'cull' of all remaining examples, although this proposal was thankfully abandoned at a later date.

However, several Phantoms have been scrapped in recent years – either due to museums closing or inspections finding the airframes to be so corroded that they were deemed unsafe. As of September 2017 just over 20 aircraft were still extant, along with several cockpit sections, although some are not on public display.

The nose section of FGR.2 XV490 receives admiring glances at one of the Newark Air Museum's popular Cockpit Fest events. *NAM via Howard Heeley*

XV424 has been at the RAF Museum, Hendon since November 1992. In 1979 this aircraft was painted in a special scheme to mark the anniversary of Alcock & Brown's 1919 crossing of the Atlantic [see p36] but is preserved in its 'normal' 56 Sqn markings. *Steve Bridgewater*

XT914 served with 14, 56, 74 and 92 Sqns as well as 228 OCU. Following retirement it was originally put on display as RAF Brampton's gate guard. When the base closed in 2012 the aircraft moved to Wattisham to form part of the Wattisham Heritage Museum.

PHANTOM SURVIVORS

SERIAL	TYPE	OWNER/LOCATION
XT596	FG.1	Fleet Air Arm Museum, RNAS Yeovilton, Somerset
XT597	FG.1	Everett Aero, Bentwaters, Sussex
XT863	FG.1	Cliftongrade Ltd, Cowes, Isle of Wight (Nose Section Only)
XT864	FG.1	Ulster Aviation Society, Long Kesh, County Antrim
XT891	FGR.2	RAF Coningsby, Lincolnshire (Gate Guard)
XT899	FGR.2	Kbely Aviation Museum, Prague, Czech Republic
XT903	FGR.2	RAF Museum Cosford, Shropshire (Nose Section Only) (Stored)
XT905	FGR.2	Everett Aero, Bentwaters, Sussex
XT907	FGR.2	Everett Aero, Bentwaters, Sussex
XT914	FGR.2	Wattisham Heritage Museum, Wattisham Camp, Suffolk
XV399	FGR.2	Privately owned, Aust-Agder, Norway (Nose Section Only)
XV401	FGR.2	Bentwaters Cold War Museum, Bentwaters, Suffolk
XV402	FGR.2	Private Owner, UK (Nose Section Only)
XV406	FGR.2	Solway Aviation Museum, Carlisle Airport, Cumbria
XV408	FGR.2	Tangmere Military Aviation Museum, Tangmere, West Sussex
XV409	FGR.2	Falkland Islands Museum, Port Stanley, Falkland Islands (Nose Section Only) (Stored)
XV411	FGR.2	Defence Fire Training and Development Centre, Manston, Kent (Hulk)
XV415	FGR.2	RAF Boulmer, Northumberland (Gate Guard)
XV419	FGR.2	Private Owner, UK (Nose Section Only)
XV424	FGR.2	RAF Museum, Hendon, Greater London
XV426	FGR.2	Mick Jennings, City of Norwich Aviation Museum, Horsham St. Faith, Norfolk (Nose Section Only)
XV460	FGR.2	Private Owner (on loan to Bentwaters Cold War Museum, Bentwaters, Suffolk
XV470	FGR.2	RAF Akrotiri, Cyprus (Stored)
XV474	FGR.2	Imperial War Museum, Duxford, Cambridgeshire
XV490	FGR.2	Mike Davey/Phantom Preservation Society, Newark Air Museum, Nottinghamshire (Nose Section Only)
XV497	FGR.2	Private Owner (on loan to Bentwaters Cold War Museum, Bentwaters, Suffolk
XV499	FGR.2	Privately owned, Bruntingthorpe Aerodrome, Leicestershire (Nose Section Only)
XV581	FG.1	ATC Aberdeen Wing, Bridge of Don Barracks, Aberdeen, Scotland (Nose Section Only)
XV582	FG.1	RAF Leuchars, Fife, Scotland [pending move to RAF Cosford – see p60]
XV586	FG.1	RNAS Yeovilton, Somerset
XV591	FG.1	RAF Museum Cosford, Shropshire (Nose Section Only)
ZE359	F-4J(UK)	IWM Duxford, Cambridgeshire (displayed as US Navy 155529)
ZE360	F-4J(UK)	Defence Fire Training and Development Centre, Manston, Kent (Hulk)
ZE350	F-4J(UK)	Privately owned, Royal Tunbridge Wells, Kent (Nose Section Only)
ZE352	F-4J(UK)	Privately owned, Hooton Park, Merseyside (Nose Section Only)
DB001	FGR.2	Newark Air Museum, Winthorpe, Nottinghamshire (Simulator/Nose Section Only)
Unknown	F-4J(UK)	Yorkshire Flight Centre, Arkendale, Knaresborough, Yorkshire (Simulator/Nose Section Only)

Left: The Imperial War Museum's F-4J(UK) Phantom was built in 1967 as BuNo155529 and entered service with the US Navy in March 1968 as an F-4J. It flew combat missions over Vietnam in 1972 but was eventually converted to meet UK specifications and transferred to the RAF as ZE359. It is seen here shortly after arriving at Duxford in 1991 – demonstrating the slightly blue hue worn by many F-4J(UK) airframes. **Right:** Prior to being ensconced in the American Air Museum at IWM Duxford, conservation staff painted ZE359 in the US Navy markings it had worn on operational missions during the Vietnam War.

Left: XV406 started life as a trials aircraft and then flew with most of the RAF's Phantom units (including 23, 29, 43, 54 and 111 Sqns). Upon its retirement it was flown to Carlisle Airport and placed on gate guard duties before eventually being passed to the resident Solway Aviation Museum. *KEY – Steve Fletcher* **Right:** Phantom FGR.2 XV474 was the first RAF F-4 to appear in the air defence grey scheme and was later acquired by the Old Flying Machine Company at Duxford. OFMC's Mark Hanna had flown the type in the RAF and was keen to maintain XV474 in airworthy condition. When Mark was killed in 1999 the plan died with him and the aircraft's ownership was subsequently transferred to the Imperial War Museum. Here, it appears alongside a Lightning in one of the museum's hangars. *Steve Bridgewater*

PHANTOM SURVIVORS

XT595 was built as one of the YF-4K prototypes for the Royal Navy and first flew in 1966. In 1988 the aircraft was delivered to the Fleet Air Arm Museum at Yeovilton, Somerset by Roger Searle and Mike Nicholl. It is seen here being handed over to museum Director Capt W J Flindell. *All KEY Collection unless stated*

XT595 is the oldest surviving British Phantom and is now displayed as part of a take-off diorama in the Fleet Air Arm Museum's Carrier exhibition.

FGR.2 XT864 on gate guardian duties at RAF Leuchars. The aircraft has since moved to North Ireland for display at the Ulster Aviation Society.

XT864 was moved by road from Scotland to Northern Ireland in 2015 and can now be seen at the Ulster Aviation Society.

This simulator is part of the collection of Phantom memorabilia on display at the Newark Air Museum in Nottinghamshire. *Steve Bridgewater*

The mortal remains of XV411 on the fire dump at RAF Manston, Kent. The aircraft moved to the airfield's Defence Fire Training and Development Centre in 1991.

Left: Seen here in the colours of 56 Sqn in the 1970s, XT891 was a 'twin sticker' and was repaired and returned to service after several incidents, including two fires and a runway crew ejection in 1984 when directional control was lost [see p76]. On retirement it became the gate guardian at RAF Coningsby. *Airspace Images* **Right:** Following its allocation to Coningsby as a gate guard, XT891 was restored to its 1968 configuration and colour scheme. It remains at Coningsby to date but is not visible from outside the base.

Nature Calls

happy reading!
Jules

This book belongs to

Heather and Ronnie

On the Isle of Wight, we have Red Squirrels and a healthy Water Vole population. Most of the plants and animals you see in this book can be seen all over the UK – all you have to do is look carefully and creep around quietly like a mouse. What can you see near your house?

For my big bruv x

The boring stuff

First published by Scarlett Inc in 2016

Text and illustration copyright © Jules Marriner 2016

The author/illustrator asserts the moral right to be identified as the author/illustrator of the work. All rights reserved. No part of this publication may be reproduced, stored in a retrieval system or transmitted in any form or by any means without the prior permission of the author/illustrator.
The author reserves the right to finish any packets of custard creams that are left lying around.

The fun stuff!!

Visit my website: julesmarrinerbooks.com
or for more fun, my blog julesmarriner.wordpress.com
You can also follow me on twitter @julesmarriner
for waffle and twaddle.
Please share!

April brings the beautiful dawn chorus as birds twitter their favourite tunes. The first babies hatch out of their eggs and the parents spend all day looking for food for them.

Look out for tadpoles and remember to take a coat as there might be April Showers.

mermaid's purse

At the end of July many children go on holiday to the beach. This little girl has found a very interesting rock pool.

Can you see a starfish?

It's August. A warm summer evening will bring out lots of moths. These ones love the nectar in the flowers.

Before the sun sets, can you hear any grasshoppers chirrupping?

chatterchatter

September is harvest time - and not just for us.
Look! that field mouse has found a tasty nut.

Wave goodbye to the swallows. They are back off to Africa.

orange tip butterfly
flutter
squeak
rabbits
wheat
ladybirds
blackberries
field mouse
squeak!

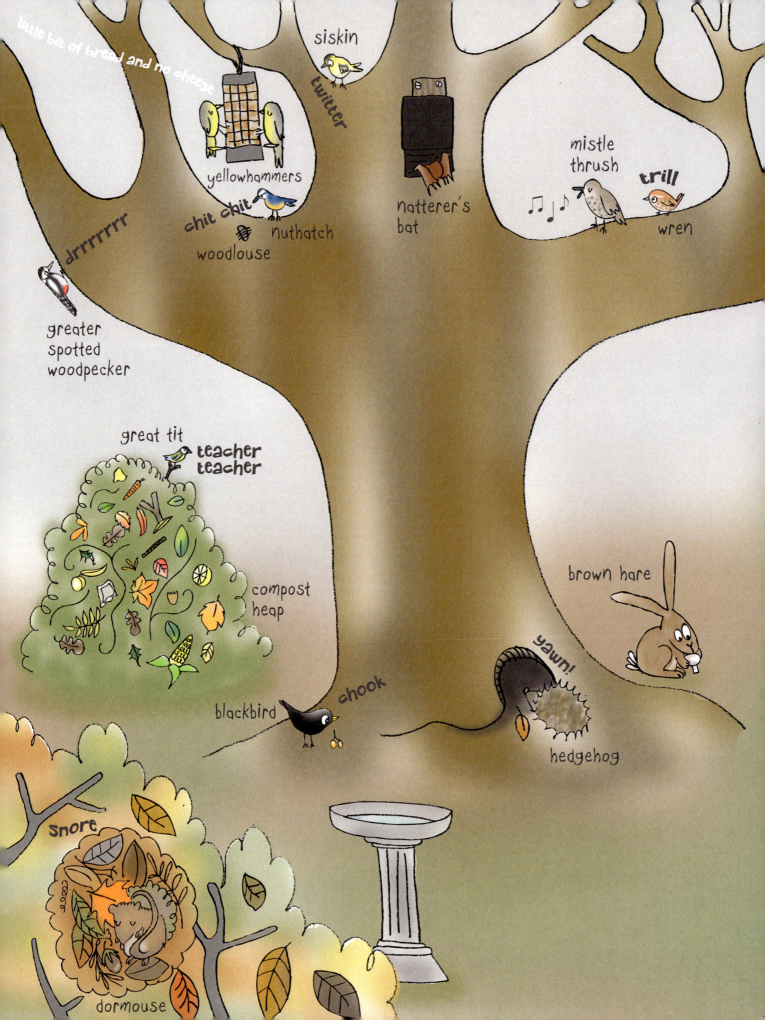

Misty mornings in November can be really chilly.

Bats, Hedgehogs and Dormice hibernate through winter but other animals come out for food on sunny winter days.

Remember to fill up your bird feeder and put out a dish of water for thirsty birds.

Have you seen.....
Tick the box if you have.

squirrel

barn owl

fox

pipistrelle bat

green woodpecker

pheasant

blue tit

garden sparrow

wren

mermaid's purse

hermit crab

sea shells

crow

buzzard

blackbird

sunflower

daisy

lavendar

TOP FACTS

The Pygmy Shrew is Britain's smallest mammal. It is the size of a man's thumb.

Young hedgehogs are called 'hoglets'.

Omnivores eat plants and animals.

Badgers take their bedding outside to air on sunny days.

Adult hedgehogs have more than 7,000 spines.

Visit our local **WILDLIFE TRUST** www.hiwwt.org.uk

A group of foxes is called a 'skulk'.

Grasshoppers can leap 20 times the length of their body.

Herbivores only eat plants.

The New Forest is at least 1,000 years old.

No. 1 Robin

The Robin was voted Britain's favourite bird in 2014.

Bees pollinate our crops; if farmers had to do this, it would cost billions of pounds.

Carnivores eat other animals.

All 16 species of bat are protected under the Wildlife + Countryside Act.

Barn Owls fly silently due to their velvety feathers.

The Queen owns all unmarked Mute swans.

The Goldcrest is Britain's smallest bird at 8cm tall.

A woodpecker pecks 20 times a second.

 There are over 3,000 types of mushroom + fungi in the U.K.

Weasels are Britain's smallest carnivore.

Each year thousands of saplings grow because squirrels have forgotten where they buried their nuts.

 Frogs and toads are gardeners' friends because they eat slugs.

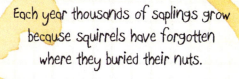

Other Books by Jules

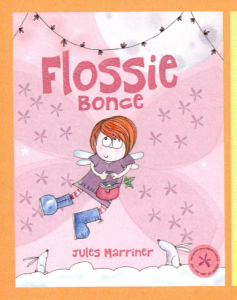
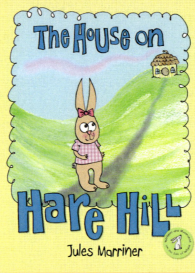
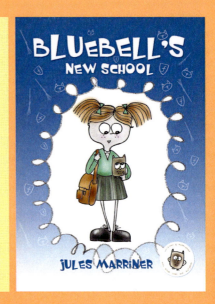
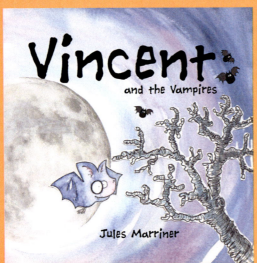
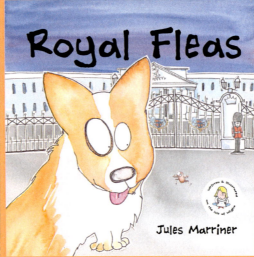

For more info including school visits :
julesmarrinerbooks.com
julesmarriner.wordpress.com
facebook.com/julesmarrinerbooks